WHAT A L

WHAT A LAUGH DOC

Dr. Isidore W. Crown

Keter Classics
London, England.

Keter Classics
37 Reid House
Bampton Road
London SE23 2BJ

First Published 2006
© Dr Isidore Crown 2006
Set in Baskerville
Cover and Production Barry Ward

A catalogue record for this book is
available from the British Library.

ISBN 0-9525373-7-0

FOREWORD

by John D. Beasley, Dip. Soc., C.Q.S.W.
Member of The Society of Authors and the Royal Historical Society

What a hoot! No book has given me more laughs than this one since I read Dr Crown's last book on his funny and bizarre experiences as a Peckham GP, Laughter is said to be good medicine so this book should improve the health of some readers.

Apart from recounting his humorous experiences in South East London, this retired doctor tells other tales which are strange but true.

For the thirty-three years I have lived in Peckham I have been a patient at the medical practice which he started in 1953, but I never saw him when I was ill. Would he have cured me by using the screwdriver he successfully used on one of his other patients?

Dr Crown's sense of humour shines through the book. His unorthodox methods demonstrated the lengths he went to while trying to help difficult people.

Isidore Crown is a compassionate man who has cared for thousands of people during the fifty years he has worked in Peckham. Since he retired in 1998 he has continued to serve local people. When one of my ears was bunged up with wax, he came to my home with his old-fashioned but effective equipment and enabled me to hear properly again - without charge.

Dr Crown, who was born in Birmingham in 1923 and qualified at King's College Hospital in 1947, is a real character; this is reflected in his experiences recorded in this appealing new book.

Countless people have benefited from this caring doctors work. It was therefore appropriate that when the practice he started, at 105 Bellenden Road in Peckham moved to new premises in Chadwick Road SE15 they were named the Isidore Crown Medical Centre.

People who have not read Dr Crown's other books have missed a treat.

Anthony Lovelock's Mother-In-Law

Anthony Lovelock was a man in his early fifties, pot-bellied, round-shouldered, grey-haired and balding. He appeared much older than his stated age and caused me all sorts of problems in May 1958.

When he did not return from work at his usual time at six o'clock one Friday evening, his wife Helen became anxious and telephoned his workplace. Anthony was a bus inspector who worked from his base at New Cross bus garage and she was told that he had left work at his usual time. She was made more anxious by the fact that Anthony was an introvert. He never went out without her or visited public houses and from the day they had married he had always gone straight home from work. None of his mates at the garage could throw any light on where he might have gone. He had said goodnight to them in the usual way. They had assumed he had gone home. When midnight came and Anthony had not gone home his wife phoned the police. They had no news of him and no hospital had been in contact with them about him. They promised to keep a look out but this was almost said to her to allay her anxiety.

Help finally came to Helen Lovelock when a middle-aged lady walking her dog through Greenwich Park on the following Tuesday went to the Greenwich police and reported a suspicious character. The man in her opinion was a pervert, a child molester or a raving lunatic. He had been sitting on the same bench for two days. He had looked quite presentable when she had first noticed him; he had winked at her, smiled and whistled after her. She had been flattered at the time, which is why she had particularly noticed him! It was evident, as she recounted her story, that no one had taken any notice of her for years as she had deliberately walked past his bench many times afterwards. He had been clean-shaven when first seen but now he had a straggly beard. He was also now dirty and unkempt, no longer a fit person to be in Greenwich Park. Indeed, when she had passed him that morning he had made funny faces, stuck his tongue out and fiddled with the fly buttons of his trousers.

The police went to the park to investigate this suspicious character on the park bench. Although Anthony refused to co-operate with them by telling them who he was they had found ample papers in his pockets to identify him. They then took Anthony home to Parkstone Road in Peckham.

Anthony had been missing for four days when I received a call from the police at 8 p.m. that Tuesday evening to visit him at his home. I had ended my surgery so had ample time to examine him thoroughly. I cannot remember whether it had rained during his escapade, but I found examining him a most unpleasant experience. He stank! The stench from his clothes hit my nostrils even before I entered the room. He must have stunk out the police car which brought him home. I had to use every artifice in my personality to prevent his wife from seeing me retching.

Anthony appeared to be suffering from amnesia. Although I had previously seen him on many occasions he did not appear to recognise me, nor did he appear to recognise his wife or mother-in-law. Maybe his non-recognition was from choice; his mother-in-law had just moved in to live with them.

I examined Anthony from head to toe. As I could find nothing wrong with him except memory loss I decided to call in a neurologist for an opinion. The neurologist was as baffled as I was. The only diagnosis I could offer the neurologist, to persuade him to do a domiciliary visit, was a mild brain haemorrhage. Anthony had never suffered from high blood pressure. None of the physical examinations fitted in with any diagnosis so the neurologist made his own diagnosis. He did not want Anthony as one of his patients! He was passed back to me to treat as I found appropriate.

Anthony's behaviour was odd. Apart from the fact that he did not seem to know who he was he also appeared to be disorientated in time and place. Now in his home environment he ate, drank and slept. Sleep perhaps was unavoidable; I kept him heavily sedated. I did not want him wandering off again before I had made some sort of diagnosis. I visited him daily for a week but he still developed no signs of any organic disorder that I could recognise. As his behaviour had not improved, and his wife had to care for his every want, I asked for a domiciliary visit from a psychiatrist. Anthony refused to leave his bed and his wife had to behave as a prison warder to prevent him from leaving the house and become lost again.

The psychiatrist came and chatted to Anthony, his wife, his mother-in-law and then me. He made the diagnosis. Anthony was suffering from an acute confusional state. His diagnosis was brilliant. He had actually put a name on what Anthony was suffering from. Anthony's wife was unimpressed. So was I!

'I could have told him what my husband was suffering from on the phone,' she said.

We now managed to get Anthony out of his bed to visit the psychiatrist. They seemed to have built up an understanding but his amnesia after several visits to him was the same as at the first home visit. No one had an answer. It was even suggested by his wife that Anthony be admitted to a mental institution!

Anthony's mother-in-law, after her husband's death in Lincoln, had come down to London to live with the couple. She had now been with them for two years and been happy until Anthony had his *turn*. She now found that she could no longer take the pressure of her son-in-law's behaviour. He had never been a bad son-in law. Her daughter had previously been able to devote all her attention to her. Now with Anthony's illness she had her hands full. The mother-in-law had to play second fiddle! She therefore decided to return to Lincoln and live with another daughter.

She left. Anthony then made a miraculous recovery! To be fair to the man it still took a week or so for his amnesia to disappear completely, but his memory did return.

Whether Anthony had a genuine cerebral vascular leak that had damaged his brain, or mother-in-lawitis, I have never been sure.

Army Tales

My practice in Peckham was founded in 1953; just eight years after the war had ended. I had been in the army myself, a medical officer in the Royal Army Medical Corps, so I was interested in many of the stories which patients told me of their army service. I had been one of the lucky ones. I had been a medical student in the war years and was not 'called up' until I had qualified. My posting had been to Neumünster, in Germany, in 1948, and I had spent my whole time in the army, in the same location, until demobilised in April 1950. I was already married when I was sent abroad and remember the chagrin felt by all the medical officers when we returned from our fortnight leave before being posted. The army was already demobilising medical officers from stations all over the world and we had been asked to volunteer before going on leave for these postings. There were exactly thirteen of us in the group; all the single men naturally volunteered for the overseas postings. The notice board, which greeted us on our return from leave, spelt out that the army knows best. All the single officers were given a home posting and all the married ones sent abroad!

National service was still in force in the 'fifties and Mike was a young single man when he served in 1950 in Malaysia, or Malaya as it was then called. He was on active service and caught up in the fight against the communists. The Chinese communists were the only effective opposition during the Japanese occupation. They were in the field and armed when the Japanese surrendered and were attempting to take over the country. They continued their guerrilla operations after the war ended. Private Mike S. was one of our many soldiers stationed in Malaya to keep them at bay and allow a legitimate government consolidate its position. He was stationed in Jahore Baru, near Singapore, but claims to have marched the whole length and breadth of Malaya during his army service.

He was a virgin soldier when he left the United Kingdom and on leave one day decided that he had been virgin long enough. His friends had chided him unmercifully about his celibacy, opportunity was plentiful in Malaya to remedy this. One day, he was persuaded to visit the red light district in Kuala Lumpur, the capital city of Malaya, to cure this condition. His friends informed him that he would return a wiser and more intelligent man after the experience.

He duly went to Kuala Lumpur, went to the red light district, and propositioned a girl there. He was in uniform and although the girls who worked the area knew that it was out of bounds to the troops what did they care? They were not going to be punished if found entertaining a soldier and could always charge more for their services to the 'services'.

The girl, who to his surprise was young and good-looking, took him to a room on the ground floor of a dilapidated house in the run-down area of Kuala Lumpur. He paid his fee for her services, she drew the curtains, and he undressed. As his friends had warned him that he would be on a 'charge' if he contracted an infection he had taken the precaution of taking a condom with him. Completely naked, with his penis as hard as a rock, with the contraceptive sheath half on and half off, there was a knock on the door.

The girl was already lying naked on the bed waiting for him. At this point, as Mike was relating this story to me, he could not contain himself and burst out laughing.

'What a situation to be in on your first time doc!' he said.

He was sweating like a pig, but as the temperature in Kuala Lumpur was ninety degrees Fahrenheit he could not remember whether it was due to the weather or general worry over the situation.

The girl jumped up to see the reason for the knock and quickly putting on a dressing gown opened the door.

'Redcaps!' she shouted. Redcap was the well-known name for the military police.

The girls who worked the district, the redcaps, and the troops in the immediate area were not the only ones who knew that the red light district in Kuala Lumpur was out of bounds to British troops - Mike also knew!

He was not however without initiative. Completely naked, he grabbed his cap, trousers, shirt and boots, opened the window and jumped out. Being naked gave him a head start. He easily managed to outstrip the Redcaps chasing him. Even today however he bemoans the loss of his money.

'I lost my money, not my virginity,' he moans.   He does however boast.

'I must be one of the very few chaps chased by the Redcaps completely naked, holding my cap, shirt, trousers and boots in one hand, and a sweaty French letter in the other'.

Mr Norton moved to Camberwell Grove, a prestigious road in Camberwell in 1945, and lived in the house until the day he died. I first met him in 1954 when Mr Brean, the local chemist, whom I had known whilst working as a trainee assistant in Colindale in 1950, introduced him to me. The reason for the introduction was that Mr Norton's son Patrick had glandular fever and as he was dissatisfied with the treatment he was receiving, transferred his family on to my medical list.

Mr Norton was born in Brooklyn, New York, in 1912, and admitted to being a tearaway as a young lad. When a young boy of fourteen he had run away to sea as a cabin boy. The first port the ship had docked in was Liverpool so he decided to remain in this country. His wanderlust however had not disappeared for he moved on to Scotland, and never idle, he had little difficulty in finding employment. His description of the country was so wonderful that his family in New York decided to come over and join him. Unfortunately, although he had settled down, they could not do so. They did not like the life in Scotland so went back to America. As he refused to join them they left him to live on his own. The wanderlust was still in his blood and he moved to London where he found employment as a moulder in an iron factory, then as a butcher, finally as a labourer.

In 1938, he joined the International Brigade, who were fighting for the Republicans against the Fascists in Spain. It was there he obtained the military experience that served him so well when fighting for this country in France in 1940. The reason he went to Spain was not political, it was that he was friendly with an Irishman from Tipperary. In his own words, 'we knocked about together', and decided to join the Spanish Republican Army as something of an adventure. They stayed together until fighting the Fascists in the Pyrenees when they were separated. He has never seen or heard of this man again. He believes the man must have been killed in action for he made every effort in this country to find him after his Spanish adventure. In any event, his sojourn in Spain lasted only six months; he was forced to flee the victorious army of General Franco and return to England.

He could find no regular employment on his return so volunteered to join the British Army. He now had a problem. He was not of British birth so was prevented from joining a regular service corps. He was however allowed to join the Pioneer Corps and served as a regimental policeman.

He was sent to France in October 1939, with no rifle, no ammunition, no military training, but with a set of toothbrushes. These toothbrushes proved to be invaluable in 1940 when the Germans in Boulogne captured him.

The first time he handled a rifle in France was when one was thrust into his hand when the Germans attacked Boulogne in 1940. He was told to use it as best he could! His previous experience in Spain now came to his rescue otherwise he would not have known how 'to load the blessed thing.'

His unit never had a ghost of a chance against the German tanks. He was wounded and taken prisoner. With another 150 prisoners of war, penned like cattle in Boulogne railway station for four days without food, they were force-marched through France and Belgium until they reached a prisoner of war camp in Germany.

On occasions, they were so hungry, they would boil bulrushes collected from the roadside in a tin helmet, to make soup. This strange macabre diet caused poisoning so diarrhoea became the norm rather than the exception.

He had been wounded in the spine in the battle for Boulogne; this finally led to paralysis from the waist down and he was hospitalised for many months. His condition deteriorated to such an extent that it was considered he might not recover so was admitted to a German hospital in Cologne. He was now under the care of German doctors but could not complain at the way he was treated during the three months that he was a patient there. Unfortunately, as he did not improve and the Germans had no intention of continuing to use their scarce precious medical resources on a prisoner of war he was transferred to a camp in Buckholt. This was more or less a holding camp that kept patients who were regarded as serious enough to be sent back home.

One day a doctor from Sweden, whom he had previously met, was passing through the hospital of the camp and private Norton complained of the treatment he was receiving. 'That goon there,' he said, pointing to a German doctor, 'called two orderlies to whip me out of bed and give me two crutches. He insisted they get me to walk. You know my case. You know I can't!'

He saw the Swedish doctor reprimand the German doctor and private Norton seeing that the moment was opportune said, 'Call this a hospital? There are no sheets. Look at the pillows! Even the hessian mattresses are filled with straw.'

That evening, every one of the patients received sheets and pillowcases.

From Buckholt he was transferred to a prisoner of war camp near the Dutch border. As he was still not able to walk and had to be carried everywhere by two other soldiers he was transferred to Obermann prisoner of war camp. For the first time he was now treated by English doctors.

The Red Cross then became involved and he is the only person I know who was repatriated by them in October 1943, from Seela to Sweden. From Sweden he went on a Red Cross train to a hospital ship *The Empress of Russia* that sailed to Scotland.

A German seaplane accompanied the boat during the whole journey from Sweden to Scotland. From Scotland he was transferred to a hospital in Sheffield for treatment. He was finally discharged from the Forces on medical grounds in January 1944.

While a prisoner of war he was in fourteen different camps but as we were relating of events which took place so long ago he had forgotten their names.

His release from the army ended his longing for adventure and a new life opened up for him. He became conservative in his outlook and a diamond polisher in Hatton Garden. He spent the next thirty years of his life there until he retired. Mr Norton is now with most of his comrades.

May his dear soul rest in peace.

Grandma and granddad Hedge were well known to my children: perhaps it was for their good nature, perhaps for their friendliness, but more likely for the provision of chocolate whenever they met.

Granddad Hedge when he retired in 1963 became my gardener and the habit of giving chocolate now invaded my house. He never appeared at my home without a bar of chocolate in his pocket for the children. He loved children, had patience beyond measure, would sit on the steps in the garden and tell my two younger children - Simon aged six and Shani aged three - stories of his exploits in the First World War. When my daughter became bored she would go to her swing. He would follow to push and while pushing continue with his story telling. He would get carried away with his memories. He was probably only too pleased to have a captive audience. When the stories became too tiresome, or the children were bored, they would run back into the house. He would then sit on one of the stones on the rockery, mop his brow, sigh, take out one of his tins of tobacco, and slowly roll himself a cigarette. He would light up, and stare malevolently at the two poplar trees at the bottom of the garden. The pattern never changed. Every time he came he followed the same routine. My garden was part of his life. He came every week on Wednesday morning at precisely the same time. There were times in his story telling when he forgot the children's ages and my son still remembers granddad's horror stories of the blood and muck in the trenches.

I knew Mr Hedge had served in the cavalry but did not know, until enlightened by my children, that the cavalry in the 1914-18 war had also fought in the trenches. My children at times were so fascinated they would ask him questions. He would elaborate, and almost certainly exaggerate to prolong the conversation. He told them that he had, with his own eyes, witnessed soldiers who had left the trenches to charge the enemy with bayonets fixed having their heads shot off. Their bodies however, rifles in their arms, bayonets fixed, continued to charge the enemy. I was pestered by my children to explain this phenomenon. The explanation of the behaviour of a decerebrate animal that one learns when studying biology in school was too difficult to explain to children of such tender years. They preferred to believe in the supernatural. What amazed me was their lack of anxiety or fright over most of these horror stories. I believe these happenings appeared to them in the realm of nursery rhymes - Three Blind Mice, Jack and Jill, Humpty Dumpty - where violence is the norm.

What really plagued granddad were the two poplars which grew on either side of my back garden, and which shaded it. They were so tall he would moan and grumble about their size. He was old and so were they. As he could not, because of his age, cut them down he could only stand and hate them while they rustled their branches in mockery. He cursed and cursed. One day his curses bore fruit. The trees were attacked by a mushroom-type growth that eventually killed them. When he first found that they had been attacked his joy was unbounded: it was as if he had won a famous victory.

When grandma Hedge died granddad was in his eighties, but as he was still a robust fellow and anxious to work I allowed him to continue as our gardener. Now at least he did not have the poplars to blight his life. It has to be pointed out however that whenever he went into the garden he first looked at the back to see whether some evil spirit had resurrected his enemy. He always carried out the same routine. Before pottering about, with his eyes firmly fixed on the back wall of the garden, he would sit down on one of the stones in the rockery and pensively smoke a cigarette.

Within six months of his wife's demise he developed a cough and I sent him for a chest X-ray. This showed a neoplastic growth, but in view of his age decided not to tell him the diagnosis and allowed him to continue work as normal. I took the precaution however of telling his family and they agreed, as intensive investigations would not provide a cure, to let him continue his normal routine.

Eight years after the growth had been found I referred him for another X-ray examination and the radiologist reported that the growth had only marginally increased in size. Granddad told me he had never felt better in his life. He still smoked, still coughed, but had never felt well while the poplars stood at the bottom of my garden. His cough was due to them. Not having to work in the shade under those accursed poplars had made all the difference to his health. He would never have had to be X-rayed if they hadn't been there. I had never met anyone who was allergic to poplars but there was always the exception. It would not however have explained his cancer of the lung. I never argued with him. After all, as he was fond of telling me, he came from Somerset. They knew of such goings on there!

Granddad lived until he was ninety, when he had a stroke, and departed this life.

———————

Mr Ernest Sharples walked into my consulting rooms one day, saw my army group photograph hanging on the wall, looked at me and said, 'Boyce Barracks, Crookham.'

This photograph had been taken in 1948 when I first joined the army during my six weeks 'square bashing' - and I asked him how he knew. He had recognised the officers in the photograph, he had been posted to Crookham himself in October 1946. As he had established himself as a fellow comrade I asked him how he had come to be in my regiment and he gave me his life history.

He was born in Wolstanton, a village in North Staffordshire, in 1928. After leaving school, having difficulty in finding suitable employment, he decided to come to London where work could more easily be found. At that time work was not all that easy to be found even in London. He was therefore not disappointed to be called up for army service in October 1946.

Private Sharples, Army No. 19090789, did his basic training in Maidstone with the Royal West Kent Regiment. He then applied and was accepted, after taking an examination, for the Royal Army Medical Corps. He did six weeks basic training in Crookham - where I had been stationed and where the photograph on the wall had been taken - and had then volunteered for duty in Palestine.

He sailed from Liverpool in January 1947 but the boat instead of sailing direct to Palestine docked first in Egypt, at Port Said. From Port Said he was transferred to the base depot at El Ballah, then posted to the British Military Hospital in Haifa.

He will never forget the journey from El Kantara in Egypt to Haifa. He was in an army train and the perfume of orange blossom on crossing the border from Sinai into Palestine was so heady as to be intoxicating. He also found exciting the novelty of children tossing huge Jaffa oranges into their train as it passed through Gaza.

The British Military Hospital had belonged to the Italian monks before the British acquired the building, but in their possession it had only been a small building with a hundred beds. This had been much too small for British requirements; they had extended the building and added extra medical and surgical beds. Some of the wards were housed in Nissan huts in the hospital grounds, the remainder in a compound, adjacent to the main building. The main building housed the operating theatre and support departments. These included dispensary, blood bank, X-ray examination rooms and dental department. The rest of the main building was divided into offices and other ranks' surgical wards.

The compound, adjacent to the main building, contained the medical wards, pathology laboratory, staff (other rank billets), quartermaster stores and NAAFI. It also contained a cinema, which doubled for shows as a theatre.

The mortuary at the time was already inadequate for their needs. It had only one slab so a much larger one was built in the grounds - at a distance from the main building.

Shortly after he arrived, the Irgun (Israeli freedom fighters) blew up the Iraqi Petroleum Company's refinery in the port area. The time was early in 1947; it had obviously been done for his benefit - to acclimatize him to the conflict.

Immediately after this a police station at Kingsway was attacked and there were many casualties. The casualties were civil police. They did not come to their hospital but to the government hospital in the lower port area, at Kyatt. A catapult, mounted on the back of a canvas-covered van, had made the attack on the police station.

The missile, an oil drum packed with explosives with an impact detonator, had scored a direct hit on the building. It had been propelled up a ramp; by this means it had shot high into the air which had enabled it to clear the ten-foot high security fence. It had landed against the wall of the building, completely blowing out the front.

He believed the attack by the Irgun on the 4th May 1947 against the crusader fortress at Acre - which was being used by the British as a prison - was carried out when the prisoners were on afternoon exercise. The fortress, when in Ottoman hands, had successfully withstood a siege by Napoleon's forces in 1799. It was no easy target! It was no mean feat the Irgun was attempting. Some explosives had obviously been smuggled into the prison beforehand. The object of the exercise was to obtain the release of Irgun prisoners held in the jail by demolishing part of the prison wall, from the inside.

The Irgun assault on the fortress had been a finely coordinated operation. Thirty men of the Irgun, a number of members of the Stern gang, and many Arab prisoners too, managed to escape. A group of British soldiers in the vicinity engaged the attackers. In the ensuing battle nine men of the Irgun were killed.

Private Sharples had been rushed to the scene from base hospital in Haifa with a six-ambulance accompaniment, but there was little they could do; most of the casualties were dead. The incident is clearly set in his memory. After the last of the ambulances had crossed the open country the Irgun blew up the road behind them which led to Acre. In this incident there were many casualties.

The common jargon in their mess was, ' If your number is on the bloody missile there is no escape.' One poor young lad had both his feet blown off having just arrived in Haifa. His number had been on that missile!

A major in the Royal Army Service Corps was brought into the hospital one day with an impacted fracture of the skull. Fortunately for him at the time there was only superficial brain damage. The skull fragments were removed and the space packed. Later the dental technician made a plate which was sutured into the skull. When the hair was combed back the scar was invisible. They were all absolutely delighted.

Unfortunately they had forgotten their mess jargon. The major's number had really been on the original missile. Either in its trajectory the missile had lost its aim or in its long travel to him had forgotten his number. The major had recovered. Two weeks after his discharge another missile did not make the same mistake. The major was shot in the chest and died on his way to hospital. Incidentally, the plate in the major's skull had been so meticulously made by the dentist it was removed at the post mortem to be used again for someone whose real number had not been on a missile.

On numerous occasions the hospital staff were called in the middle of the night to help unload, and transport, injured Jewish immigrants from Royal Navy ships which had intercepted the immigrant boats trying to enter Palestine illegally. The concern he and his friends felt when they had to deal with these people was indescribable. They felt so sorry for these poor devils that had suffered unimaginable trials and tribulations in German concentration camps only to be apprehended within sight of their 'Promised Land.' Amongst the ships he saw escorted into Haifa was the ship featured in the book *Exodus* by Leon Uris.

The ships carrying the refugees were mostly dilapidated, junkyard, boats of all shapes and sizes. Most of them were not fit to be on the Thames, never mind a sea journey! When apprehended by the navy they were escorted into Haifa and tied up in the harbour facing the hospital cinema. They were a constant reminder to the hospital staff of man's inhumanity to man!

As soon as the watermelons came into season the hospital wards filled up. There were widespread attacks of typhoid fever whilst he was in Haifa and they were also hit by an epidemic of cholera brought in from Egypt. On one occasion they even had an attack of bubonic plague. Whenever an epidemic was prevalent the cinema was closed and all the troops in north Palestine were brought in to them for inoculation.

When Palestine was finally partitioned by the United Nations on 24th November 1947 he and the rest of the troops breathed a sigh of relief. There would now be peace. They could all go home. They were not politicians. They really thought that peace would reign. How wrong they were! The Jews and Arabs, instead of fighting the British, now fought each other. Jewish buses and cars were now covered with armour and all the seats except those of the drivers' were removed.

The hospital could now watch the struggle between Jew and Arab. The boundary fence of the medical compound bordered the Tel Aviv to Haifa road; on the other side of the fence was an Arab garage. The British knew that this garage specialised in making armoured cars - to attack the Egged (Jewish) buses which used the road - but did not hamper the construction. The Jews however were determined to keep this main road open at all costs. One night they attacked the garage with hand grenades and a Piat anti-tank gun. Though the battle was on their doorstep the British made no attempt to interfere. The noise however gave them a sleepless night.

A few months before the British finally pulled out of Palestine Ernest Sharples was faced with his own personal problems. He spilled Iodine down the front of his overall by dropping a demijohn. This demijohn knocked over a primus in the dispensary igniting the iodine and poor Ernest sustained second-degree burns to his left leg. He now became a hospital patient instead of orderly, and was an invalid for several weeks. On recovering from the attack he found that he could not stand for long periods so was transferred from the dispensary to the pathology laboratory. His arrival at the laboratory was fortuitous. It coincided with an outbreak of typhoid fever, and his first tasks were to take samples of faeces from the patients' overnight bedpans.

When he was told that he was due to be demobilised he was at first delighted, until informed that he was first going to be posted to the British Military Hospital at El Ballah in Egypt. His stay however was a short one and he was transferred to a British Military Hospital in Malta. From Malta he returned to England on the good ship *Empress of Australia* in February 1949.

He had served in Palestine for two turbulent years and was delighted to return home. At times however, as the country is always in the news, he has feelings of nostalgia. He has the wish to return to see for himself what development has taken place since he was last there in 1949.

Betting Problems

My experiences with the betting fraternity had commenced when I was an assistant doctor in Newport, Monmouthshire, in 1951. Sid Joseph, a bookmaker, befriended me but that is another story in this book. My father-in-law was fond of a small bet and I remember taking him one day to Lingfield Park. But my experiences when I had all losers, except for one race, warned me off becoming a gambler.

It was only by recommendation, as his wife was an NHS patient of mine that I became acquainted with Mr Deveson, who owned the Hope public house in Rye Lane for 30 years until he retired in the 1970s. He was a character of the old school. He was always immaculately dressed in the height of fashion and wore a bow tie. He was never lost for lady admirers. When I first got to know him it never stretched my imagination to believe all the stories of his being a *lady-killer*.

I first knew him when he was already in his sixties and still a very handsome man with a charming personality. Before he had bought the Hope, he had lived with his parents in the Bun House in Peckham High Street which his father had owned since 1911. The Bun House had some interesting traditions that had been initiated in 1920 and continued until 1960. On Christmas Day the carver, from Simpson's in the Strand, came specially to carve the turkey.

Another tradition, on New Year's Day the poor people in the community were given a free dinner consisting of boiled beef, carrots, pease pudding and a piece of crusty bread. All were welcome. No questions were asked. Dinner was served from eleven in the morning until three o'clock in the afternoon. The area has never been short of poor people so the walls of the Bun House on New Year's Day were bursting at the seams. The owner of the Bun House was well known in the community for his charitable work and his son, the fellow I knew, followed in his father's footsteps. No one who entered his bar in the Hope in need of a few shillings ever left empty handed.

Whilst ninety-nine per cent of the customers of the Hope did not have the wherewithal to own an old jalopy the owner drove a Rolls Royce. What was so peculiar about this man, whose friends were working-class Peckhamites, was that he did not have an ounce of pomposity in him. He treated his friends as equals although he paid all the expenses.

Many of my patients frequented his bar daily in the morning to place their bets with the bookie's runner. At that time horse and dog race betting was illegal except at the racetrack or by telephone so the bookie's runner sat or stood at the public bar collecting bets. Although everyone knew the transactions were illegal his trusted clients surreptitiously slipped bits of paper into his hand with their bets and money. He took these to the bookmaker's office. Winners were paid in the bar on the following day - just as illegally. Interestingly, the police turned a blind eye most of the time. I know as a fact that he was tipped off when they intended to raid the bar and arrest some punters.

Mr Deveson was also an amateur jockey and owned two race horses. He could often be seen at the racetrack riding his own horses. He rarely won but was such a sportsman that he went only for the ride. Another of his pursuits was to go to the Serpentine in Hyde Park with his friends on Christmas Day to break the ice and take a dip.

When he retired, it was said by the local fraternity that the last bit of old-fashioned life in Rye Lane died with him. Unfortunately, this has indeed proved to be so!

The Secret Life Of Charlie Perkins

It was an ice-cold day in January 1953. I had been in practice in Peckham for only four days when Mr Charles Perkins came in to see me. He had been on the list of my predecessor Dr Morgan and, although he had been receiving treatment from the locum practice since Dr Morgan's retirement, had decided to try a new, friendlier face.

Charlie Perkins was an ailing man in his middle fifties who suffered from rheumatoid arthritis, asthma, chronic bronchitis and emphysema. He was therefore a regular attendee at the surgery. I can even remember the first prescription I gave him; it was for a new asthma pump, and rybarvin solution to put into it, to relieve his wheezing.

He was married, with two teenage children, and lived in Lyndhurst Way around the corner from the surgery. When the family moved to a house in Crystal Palace Road in 1956 he found the walk to the surgery just that little bit too far. He then came to the surgery in his van, which he parked outside. This was before the days of yellow lines and parking meters. Few people in Peckham owned cars and there was always ample parking space when he came to see me.

I often wondered why he owned a van but thought it impolite at the time to ask him. In any case it was none of my business. I thought perhaps he was borrowing his employer's van but if so I could not understand why there were no markings or advertisements on it. No one who saw this van could have guessed for what purpose it was being used.

One day, on returning from a visit just before commencing evening surgery, I found it parked in the street and blocking the entrance to the surgery. I was not too pleased. He had expropriated my parking space. As I passed, I noticed that there was a noticeable smell coming from inside the van. I stopped, and wondered where I had previously encountered this odour. I remembered.   I had helped my *Zeida* (grandfather) in the *schechthouse* (slaughter house) as a young boy. I have never forgotten that smell.

My *Zeida*, a man in his eighties, had been a *shochet* (ritual slaughterer) of chickens: I had accompanied him on numerous occasions and watched while he worked. He had been most particular not to cause any suffering to a bird. Not only had he been an extremely religious man he had been a professional one too. The duty of a shochet is to slaughter an animal or bird without causing pain or distress. When on the occasion due to age he thought his hand trembled a little, and he might have caused suffering, he retired on the spot. He was eighty-two years old at that time.

The smell in the chicken house was the same smell as emanated from the van, but rather than embarrass Mr Perkins I refrained from mentioning the stench. I did not have the heart to tell him that his van had a fowl, foul smell.

Charlie Perkins continued to see me regularly in the surgery until 1969 when he had an attack of influenza and was forced to take to his bed. As he suffered from chronic bronchitis the influenza floored him. He was very ill so I was asked to visit him at home.

During the whole time I was in his house the telephone in the living room, which was next to his bedroom, never stopped ringing. It was answered by his wife who appeared to be writing out orders and was evidently using the living room as an office. I examined Mr Perkins, prescribed for him, then told him that he would have to remain in bed for a few days and that I would revisit. I forbade him to make any attempt to return to work.

Whilst in the bedroom, I could often hear his wife in the room next door saying on the phone, 'Yes, Mrs Cohen. No, Mrs Cohen.'

I was intrigued. I asked Charlie Perkins what his business was and pretended that this would have some bearing on the length of time that he was housebound. He looked at me for a few minutes without answering then, as I stood by his bed not making any effort to leave, he told me his story.

He was a poultry man who bought chickens from a farm in Kent and delivered them to his customers in his van. He dealt only with dead birds, never, ever, with live ones. When specially ordered he delivered eggs as well.

'If you are doing a delivery service why don't you advertise?' I asked.

He began to laugh so heartily - which triggered off a bout of wheezing and coughing - I thought he would require resuscitation before he would be able to continue. 'If I advertised,' he finally managed to blurt out, 'I would be bankrupt in a week.'

I looked at him in disbelief. 'Why?'

'I will tell you if I can swear you to secrecy,' he answered.

I promised. He told me. His business was delivering poultry and eggs to his Jewish customers in North West London. He had only wealthy clients. They were always giving parties, his business was a flourishing one. Most of his customers pretended to be observant, to lead good, kosher lives. 'You have now guessed why I have no markings on my van. My poultry is not kosher.'

He elaborated. His business was run strictly by telephone and recommendation. He always delivered his poultry by the back door - never the front! Always to the lady herself - never to the maid or au pair. If the maid answered the door, he asked for the lady of the house. If she was not in, he gave the maid a dozen eggs, told her the lady had ordered them, and he would come back later to see the lady for payment. This gave him the excuse he needed to call back and deliver the poultry. He could not leave the poultry with the maid; she was never a party to the arrangement. Indeed, the maid was always a worry to him. Should one ever become suspicious, his business could be in ruins. At that moment I thought a funny look crossed his face, but on reflection, it must have been pain from his wheezy old chest. He knew his role by heart. One stupid mistake would cost him his living. As his clients trusted him implicitly he would never betray that trust. He was not breaking any laws. He was only making a living!

The instructions from his customers were explicit. Should any rabbi or synagogue official be in the neighbourhood when he called he was to postpone his delivery until the coast was clear. He had done his homework. He had made it his duty to recognise the kosher butchers in the area, also the local rabbis and synagogue officials. His deliveries were always made very early in the morning, or when it was dark. He therefore preferred the winter; he then had longer periods for safe delivery.

He quipped, 'I have often delivered my order by the back door and as I have left have seen the kosher butcher pull up at the front.'

'Why should people bother to go to all the trouble and buy from you?' I asked.

' Well,' he answered, 'if you are not too fussy yourself and want to pretend that you eat only kosher you order meat and some fowls from the kosher butcher weekly, but get your main supply of chickens from me. Don't forget my chickens are a fraction of the price of the ones supplied by kosher butchers. My customers save pounds by buying from me. I never ever provide a bill, give a receipt, or receive cheques. Telephone calls and cash only. My whole business depends on complete and utter secrecy. As I have already said I would go bankrupt if I advertised, or if anyone not in the know found out what my business was. It has to be remembered, if anyone ever became slightly suspicious and tried to trace my van what chance would they have of following me from North West London to Peckham?'

Mr Perkins had obviously been most reluctant to tell me this story. He knew that plucking feathers was not helpful for his asthma. He also knew that I was a religious Jew.

'If this is all true, tell me the name of the rabbi in Wembley,' I said.

He had previously told me that he knew all the Jewish officials in the area which he serviced.

He didn't hesitate, 'Rabbi Myer Berman.'

I was nonplussed. He even knew his first name. I knew the rabbi. He was the brother of my aunt by marriage.

His story was true!

In 1972 Charlie Perkins made peace with the rabbis and synagogue officials of North West London. He had an attack of bronchopneumonia from which he never recovered. May his dear soul rest in peace.

His business died with him.

Christmas Day

It was normal custom in this country before the turn of the present century for a Jewish doctor - in partnership or working in a group of Christian doctors - to make himself available to be on duty on Christmas Day and to allow his colleagues the freedom of being with their families and free from worry. As I am a Jew, my partners Drs Cook and Healy would have been astonished had I even hinted that I did not expect to be on duty on that day. I must be honest, work was always light - except for the first year in my practice.

The year was 1953 I was a single-handed GP and had been in the practice for only eleven months. My family lived on the premises and I used two rooms for the small number of patients on my medical list. I had inherited only 200 patients from the previous practitioner. I must not be spiteful; he worked until his dying day, and was eighty-five years old when the Good Lord decided to take him into his keeping.

In the short time I had been in the practice I had already built up a list and was now the proud principal of 800 patients. I worked very hard in achieving this. Believing that opening for two hours on Christmas Day would enhance my recognition in the area I did a two-hour surgery (10 a.m. - 12 noon). One person was already waiting for me to open and after treating him I spent the next one hour and fifty minutes in the dining room drinking tea with my wife. I had made visits every ten minutes to the waiting room but finding it empty returned to my tea drinking sessions. At five minutes to twelve my wife told me that I should close the front door. The attempt to invite people in on Christmas Day had obviously failed.

I opened the dining room door and stood astonished. I had to fight my way past a crowd of patients who had not only filled the waiting room and corridor to it but some had been forced to find space on the stairs which led to our sleeping quarters. Nearly all were new patients. It was a very profitable day for me, but it taught me a valuable lesson. All had come with trivia and were making a visit to me to suit their convenience. All their ailments could have waited another day! This culture has helped to destroy the National Health Service. Doctors use appointment systems to curtail the number they see, the time which can be given to a patient, and the continuity of care which a doctor can give to an individual patient.

The excitement of Christmas always affected the children in my practice, although visits were rare; it was invariably to a small child.

One of the Boulter boys when last seen by me in 2003 was over six feet tall, but as a child he invariably had an asthma attack on Christmas Day. The attack I particularly remember occurred about thirty years ago when he had been given a train set as a present. He promptly had an attack and I was called to treat him. I played with him and his train set for such a long time that his mother was certain his symptoms improved more from the playmate than the medication.

On Christmas Day I made it a rule in the '70s to visit Mrs Tolputh, an old lady in her eighties who lived in Brayards Road. Her tiny house, on two floors, was situated alongside the railway embankment and was in a dilapidated condition. It had been built in the early Victorian period when houses were built to last but the passing of trains over the years had taken its toll. The fact that the landlord of her tiny dwelling had never bothered to take care of his property had not helped. Every time a train went by the windows rattled, the foundations shook, the house heaved a sigh, then returned on to its base.

The ground floor consisted of a small kitchen and a dark dining room, the window of which was only ten feet away from a grassy slope and the railway line The dining room contained the basics - a sink with a cold-water tap and a rusty gas stove. A door led from the kitchen to the miserable outside toilet which had not been refurbished from the day it had been installed.

The upstairs accommodation consisted of one room, which Mrs Tolputh used as a lounge and which also served as a bedroom. This was furnished with an armchair, a table, a single bed, two chairs, and a large wardrobe in the corner of the room. A small coal fireplace with a wood-surround completed the furnishings.

She lived alone. Although her son and his family lived only ten doors away the only contact she had with them was when her son dropped a card in her letterbox on Christmas Day. Her married son neglected her completely and had never given her the pleasure of seeing her grandchildren who were now over twenty years old. She told me that if they passed her in the road she would not recognise them. The last time she had seen them they had been babies. The reason for the neglect was that the daughter in-law did not like her. Not even to invite her on Christmas Day was beyond my comprehension!

I believed that my visit gave her a little happiness. She was such a dear sweet soul. I could not understand why her family could not show an old lady some charity on this day - even if she had at some time wronged them. I never found out when the rift had occurred or why. As her son and family were not patients of mine I had no opportunity of asking them. Poor Mum was so lonely on Christmas Day. The streets were deserted. Even the house was friendless. One could even feel tranquillity in the atmosphere. It did not vibrate to the shaking of the trains, to break the silence.

An hour or so of my time for a sherry and a chat was certainly no hardship for me on this day to give a little happiness

One year, in one of our chats, she said to me,

'Do you know, I met my son out shopping in Rye Lane a few weeks ago. I haven't come face to face with him for ten years. He looked so old. That battleaxe of a wife has certainly aged him. He was evidently shocked to see me for he said, "Good God! Mom! They told me you were dead!"'

I looked at her rather sadly, but she was not at all put out.

'I really told him. A fine son I've got! He couldn't even be bothered to come to his mother's funeral!'

Never A Dull Moment In Peckham

On a bitterly cold rainy day in January 1953, on the 12th to be exact, I commenced to practise in Peckham, in South East London.

It had been an uphill struggle in 1953 to be given a practice. All my applications for vacancies had been rejected with the excuse - lack of experience. As I write this in 2005, over fifty years later, I marvel at the lack of experience of governments. We had a surplus of general practitioners at that time, now we have to import from abroad even to maintain minimum standards. When I began to practise as a single-handed doctor in the area it was in 105 Bellenden Road, a private house, and we lived on the premises. The practice remained in the same premises until 31st July 1998, when it moved to the medical centre in Chadwick Road. I retired from the group, but continued to work privately from a flat in Forest Hill.

All the stories in this book are true. Dear reader, if you recognise yourself in one of the stories thank you for being my friend and making my life with you in Peckham such a happy one. I hope we will enjoy each other's company for many more years.

The Group Practice that left Bellenden Road on July 31st 1998 consisted of four doctors. They were Drs. Lai Cheng Wong, Michael Duggan, Anthony Stimmler and Colin Wong.

When the group was formed in 1965 it consisted of five doctors - Drs Merton Blank, A. Bhatt, William Cook, Isidore Crown and Andrew Healy. We quickly found the premises were much too small to accommodate five doctors comfortably so Dr Bhatt, who had retained his premises in Bushey Hill Road, left us. He returned there to practise single-handed until the day he retired.

From 1953 -1957 I practised completely alone and was on 24 hours duty seven days a week. There was no deputising service available and as my practice was expanding so rapidly I decided to discuss the formation of a rota service for night visits with the local doctors. They were invited with their wives to my house in Bellenden Road. This was the first occasion I met Celestine Healy, Dr Healy's wife.

Celestine was gorgeous. She was an extrovert, had a perfect figure and had most certainly kissed the Blarney Stone. She was a magnet for all the males because of her charms, but the envy and dislike of their wives.

She was a character. If she liked you she loved you. If she did not she did not hesitate to let you know. She was a genius in mockery. I have been in her company and watched people squirm in confusion as she turned her talents to their undoing.

Mrs Healy was a religious catholic and went to mass every morning. This did not however prevent her from cutting willow for me from her garden in Dulwich for the Jewish festival of Tabernacles. One story of hers always amused me.

The husband of one her friends had died. He was Jewish, but his wife was a Catholic. On his deathbed he had made two wishes. One was that he was to be cremated, and the second was that his ashes were to be scattered in a Jewish cemetery. Celestine telephoned me one day during a morning surgery knowing that I was an orthodox Jew and asked me who to contact to fulfil the fellow's last wishes. I told her I doubted that this would be possible. Cremation, I informed her, was frowned upon in Orthodox Jewish circles and the Rabbinate would certainly not give permission to have his ashes scattered in one of the cemeteries over which they had jurisdiction. I was obviously not in a position to give her a definite decision but advised her to get in touch with the United Synagogue Burial Society.

She followed my advice and telephoned the secretary. He had been courteous and friendly but told her that it was not possible for his ashes to be scattered in any of the cemeteries of his organisation. He advised her to contact the Liberal organisation. Her answer to him had been curt.

'At a time like this you have to bring politics into it!'

Sadly, our Celestine departed this life a few days after Christmas 1988. Dr Healy left this life to join her in September 2002.

———————

For the first eleven years I worked without assistance and to make ends meet I worked at night for a few years in the East End for a ten-doctor group of doctors. I had however by 1956 built up enough goodwill amongst my patients to employ a regular locum to do my surgery on Saturday morning so that I could attend the Sabbath services in the local synagogue in New Cross. As I did a normal regular Saturday evening surgery patients who wished to see me personally on that day would still be able to do so.

One Saturday in February 1962, on returning home from the Synagogue at about 12.30 p.m., I was asked by my wife to telephone the housekeeper at the surgery as she had received an urgent call. At that time in the National Health Service it was the duty for doctors either to live on the surgery premises or to employ a housekeeper to do so. We had by this time moved from the practice premises as our family had increased and the premises were too small for our growing family. We were living in Hilly Fields Crescent, Brockley about three miles from the surgery and within walking distance - if needs be.

I telephoned the housekeeper and was astonished to learn that the waiting room was full of patients. Consultations should have commenced at 9 a.m. but the doctor had disappeared almost immediately after his arrival. Many of the patients had been waiting for over three hours and were becoming restless but she did not know how to handle the situation.

'Dr Watton did not turn up then! He has never let me down before, 'I remarked.

'He turned up all right. He didn't bother to do the surgery,' was the reply.

I could not believe that I had heard correctly as the good doctor had already been paid for the morning's work. I asked her to repeat what she had said, and she did so in no uncertain terms.

Dr Watton, who had been booked to start work at 9 a.m., came in about half an hour late and appeared to be somewhat in a hurry. He had rushed through the waiting room into my consulting room and taken off his overcoat. He had then walked quickly back into the waiting room and barked:

'Hands up all those patients who are genuinely ill.'

The astonished patients were mesmerised and too shocked to answer. No one said a word, silence reigned in the waiting room.

'Oh well, if no one is genuinely ill I don't see why I should waste my time.'

He had walked back into my consulting room, put on his overcoat, said 'Good morning' to the bewildered patients sitting in the waiting room, and left the premises. Patients were still arriving but the patients in the room did not tell them of the situation as they did not know Dr Watton and thought he was playing some sort of a joke. It was not until they had become frustrated at the long wait that they had summoned the housekeeper.

I was left having to tidy up the mess that day, with no lunch and no tea. I also did not receive my money back from the locum.

―――――――

One of the patients waiting to see Dr Watton that morning who was not genuinely ill was Mr Anthony Hempson, a man in his early forties, who lived in Nutbrook Street. He was a malingerer, a nuisance, and a small-time crook who made my life a misery. Whenever I saw him I became distraught. He invariably brought on one of my migraine attacks. He practically lived in my surgery. I was sick to death of him. If it were not for the fact that almost all his neighbours were patients of mine I would have removed him from my medical list. I continued to suffer for twelve whole years, until he moved to Forest Hill and I told him that he lived too far for me to visit.

He was short, five foot nothing in height, and looked the same in width. He was broad shouldered, heavily built, and over twenty stone in weight. He was round faced, but never smiled. I tried hard many times to get a smile out of him, I was always unsuccessful. He never ever showed emotion. His wife matched him in size and temperament. It is said that animals come in pairs. Thank God they were childless.

The problem I personally had with him was that he used me for his many adventures.

He constantly found a hole to fall into or fall out of or a shop to fall into or out of. He was apparently being pushed into or out of something all the time. He was either knocked down by a car that appeared out of thin air, tripped up by, or hit by, an overhanging branch of a tree. Trees would sprout out of the ground in the most unusual places just for the purpose of injuring our poor Anthony. Protruding roots caused him years of agony, pain, and distress.

He was a lover of water. Water caused him untold injuries. With the weather in this country being rather on the moist side he revelled in it. Water mixed with earth equals mud. What slipping, sliding, and injuries could be had with this mixture! He worshipped our weather. Why not? It gave him a very good living. Another of his favourite hobbies was tangling with walls. A wall would fall on him, jump out of its natural position to hinder his passage, or suddenly appear out of thin air to wound him. Never enough to complete the job to my satisfaction! These were just a few of his favourite complaints. My predicament was that I was the unwilling listener to these complaints.

We shared a life of continuous litigation. Not a week went by without my receiving a letter demanding a report from one firm of solicitors or another. He never used one firm of solicitors for his litigation; he used a different one for each complaint. I never found out why. I would have thought that he would have saved money by using just one. Perhaps it was just to persecute me!

By using different firms of solicitors he confused me and caused me all sorts of problems. Whenever I received a letter about one of his accidents I was forced to waste my time checking through his records to match up the accident and the date with the firm of solicitors. One firm would write to me about an arm injury he had sustained one day. Another firm would write about an arm injury not too dissimilar from the first, a few days later. He was always the victim. Never ever in any circumstances could he have been the offender, or by his negligence brought about the injury.

He had learnt very quickly that almost all the defendants he threatened to take to court preferred to settle out of court than risk the expense of litigation. In this way he made a comfortable living from his accidents.

For example, following an accident to his ankle he would present himself at my surgery requiring treatment. His ankle would be swollen and deformed. It would have all the appearance of a sprain or fracture. From his moans and groans when he presented himself to me you would have believed he had suffered a major heart attack. He would - to be honest - indeed be suffering some pain but probably thought if he had to earn the money he had to act the part. On every occasion I had to take the precaution of having the offending bone or joint X-rayed so that he would not have the excuse of litigating against me too.

After the examination, he would ask me to provide him with a certificate to prove that he had suffered an injury and I honestly could not refuse. He had definitely suffered an injury, but whether sustained wilfully or accidentally was impossible to establish. There was no way any doctor could have stood in the witness box and prove the accident had been self inflicted. I was giving him a certificate only for an injury he had suffered, not giving an opinion as to how it was caused.

On leaving me he would go to a firm of solicitors with my certificate to commence proceedings against the offending party. The solicitors he had chosen for that particular case would state to the offending party that their client would be prepared to settle the claim out of court if the damages were sufficiently rewarding.

He was astute. He had plenty of experience. He obviously knew how much to ask without the defence being prepared to contest the amount in court. On one occasion the local council did prepare a defence to one of his claims when he tripped over a paving stone in Blenheim Grove. This is where Anthony's experience told. He had chosen the right stone. Another person had previously reported this paving stone as faulty and had written to complain, but having suffered no injury had made no claim. Whether the writer of the letter and Anthony were in collusion I never found out. The council however repaired the fault and settled out of court rather than fight a losing suit.

He once absent-mindedly scratched himself on a tree in the front garden of the surgery. He had obviously forgotten where he was and that I knew his game. When he came in to complain I treated him with the greatest respect. I gave him an injection against lockjaw, an injection of penicillin to prevent infection, a reprimand to watch where he walked in future, and a form to take to the optician for an eye test!

One of his favourite stunts - I had written many reports on his accidents of this type to his solicitors - was to stand up in a bus just as it was going to stop. He would hope the driver would slam the brakes on quickly and the bus would pitch forward. The more violent the lurch the better! He would arrive in my surgery immediately afterwards as an emergency with some injury or another. His arm would ache for weeks. I lost count of the number of whiplash injuries recorded in my medical records as a result of one of these lurches. Unfortunately, although lawyers may have different opinions, it is not always easy for a doctor to diagnose whether a patient has a whiplash injury, or strained ligaments as a result of a particular accident. It is of course possible these symptoms preceded the accident. To prove it however is impossible.

Fortune finally favoured me. He decided to move away from Nutbrook Street in Peckham, to Inglemere Road in Forest Hill. I plucked up courage and told him that as he and his wife were now living out of my catchment area they would have to find a new doctor.

I had suffered twelve years of misery and hell. The move had given me the excuse I had prayed for; the couple changed their doctor. I saw them once or twice afterwards whilst out shopping in Rye Lane, but purposely crossed the road before we met, in case he tripped over my foot!

Five years later I read about his escapade in the local paper. He had fallen down the stairs of a double-decker bus in Rye Lane, Peckham.

The bus had suddenly made an emergency stop to avoid hitting a pedestrian. On this occasion however his fall had been ill timed. He fell out of the bus into the road and sustained a fractured skull. He died in the ambulance on the way to hospital.

There was only one black fellow known to me in the immediate area when I moved into Peckham but by 1956 many had been recruited to work in this country from the West Indies and had settled in Peckham. A good number became patients of mine. As I liked their Victorian values, happy dispositions and sense of fun, we rapidly became friends. I was therefore not surprised when Irving, a young Jamaican lad just nineteen years old, came in to see me in 1964 as an emergency.

He had been in the country only a few months. He had come to join his parents who were working on the buses and his problem was that he had contracted a urethral discharge. The verbiage he actually used was, 'it jooks me in my thingy!'

The terminology was explicit. I knew immediately what he meant. I had already learnt a good deal of Jamaican expressions and his statement needed no clarification.

I examined him and when I told him he had a venereal infection and that I would have to send him to a special clinic for treatment he became furious. I explained to him that I was sending him so that he could be investigated and treated properly. My efforts however to appease him failed. He became angrier and angrier. Finally I asked him his reasons for feeling so annoyed at my sending him for proper treatment.

He told me that he had been solicited by a white girl at the corner of Rye Lane and Peckham High Street, outside Jones and Higgins, two days previously. She had taken him to Peckham Rye Park, charged him ten pounds for sex on the grass, and then allowed him to perform only once. Ten pounds was an awful lot of money! I could now understand why he felt so aggrieved at being told that he had an infection. He had paid her his good hard-earned money. She was white. How could she possibly have given him an infection?

His understanding was, having paid a white girl for sex, he would be free from infection. He had been sexually active in the West Indies, could not remember how many girls he had been with, had never paid anything, and never caught anything. He was furious. It did not take me long to realise from the way he was describing events that I was dealing with a real thicko.

I put on my most serious expression, which was an effort at the time, and explained that ten pounds was a lot of money for a white girl to charge for sex in a park. He had to be someone special! With tongue in cheek, I told him that never in a thousand years would I have been charged as much as this for a quickie in Peckham Rye Park. He had definitely not been overcharged. This girl had fancied him. It was obvious, besides having sex with him she had given him a present. In this case the present was gonorrhoea. He was a very lucky boy. Should she have gone overboard and found him irresistible in all probability he would have been charged twenty pounds. He would then most certainly have been given syphilis as a present. If she had charged him more than twenty pounds God only knows what devilish present she would have presented him with.

He was a very lucky boy. The lesson he had been taught was that if he had to pay for sex in this country he should do without.

At the same time as I was making my explanations, doing my best to keep a straight face, he stood looking at me open-mouthed - as though I was reading a tract from the bible. How I thanked my grandfather and rabbinical teachers for giving me a grounding in the Talmud and allowing me to argue a case without my knowing what I was talking about.

Irving, I could see, was trying with all his might to absorb what I was saying to him. He was fighting a losing battle! I don't think he understood my reasoning. In fact, I am sure he did not. He was not the only one. I did not understand it myself! His face had the same bland expression - when I had completed my recital - as when I had commenced. He was however suitably impressed. I had been successful in my nonsensical line of reasoning.

He went away with my letter to the *special clinic* in St Giles' Hospital quite happily.

———

George came to see me for the thousandth time, one evening in 1975, complaining of grating in his head. From 1969 he had driven me to distraction with this grating. No treatment of mine had been of any avail. He had come back to see me as the treatment advised by the last hospital I had referred him to had been useless. I had already sent him to six hospitals. He had tormented me so much over the years, in order to get him off my back, I had referred him to different hospitals hoping that some bright consultant might accidentally hit on a cure.

I stared at him for a few moments, looked around the room, then got up and left with the excuse that I had to see the practice manager on an urgent matter. I wanted to think, away from my torturer. I was at my wits end! My diagnosis was, still is forty years afterwards, that his symptoms were due to Eustachian tube catarrh.   As every doctor knows this condition is very difficult to treat.

George, was a small and black West Indian gentleman aged forty-nine. To his credit, in spite of his symptoms, he had taken little time off work. He was however a constant complainer, a thorn in my side, a weekly attendee at the surgery. I was never too pleased to see him. I had not given satisfaction, and his symptoms were still as troublesome to both doctor and patient as the first day he had come to see me.

I returned to my patient after having taken a little breather and opened one of the drawers in my desk to take out a book that lists all the hospitals in the London area. This had been presented to me by the Emergency Bed Service. I now intended to send him to the furthest hospital in the book with some *cock and bull* story that it was the only one left which specialised in the disease from which he was suffering.

In the drawer, my eyes fell on a screwdriver which I had evidently used for some purpose in the surgery and forgotten to take home. Years of experience in the treatment of George had already taught me that he was not too bright intellectually. I took the screwdriver out of the drawer, put it on my desk, and waited for a reaction. The screwdriver was a large one, and for the life of me I still cannot remember the reason for it being there.

There was no reaction from George. I took his head between my hands and shook it sharply several times, backwards and forwards. He offered no resistance - just allowed me to do it. I kept my hands on his head and then shook his head sharply from side to side.

'I've got it! I can hear it!' I said

I pretended to look pleased. He didn't answer, just stared at me. I looked him straight in the eyes.

'I know your trouble. They have all missed it! The screw in the deep fascia connecting your parietal and temporal bones have worked loose. Why didn't you tell me that beside the grating you had a click?'

He just sat in his chair mutely, not comprehending my question. He was obviously more lost for words than I was, so I repeated the process. I shook his head several more times, backwards and forwards, then side to side. He sat in his chair bolt upright. He allowed me to proceed without uttering a single word.

The screwdriver looked at me so lovingly that I took it and pressing it gently into the area of the temporomandibular joint (jaw), turned it a few times. I made sure that I turned it correctly, clockwise, as one would tighten a screw, so as to avoid any suspicion. He worked as a platelayer on the railway. Whatever his brainpower he would certainly know which way a screw was turned to tighten!

He did not flinch nor show any emotion. I blinded him with science. I explained what I was doing to him. I was tightening the screw that fitted into a nut inside his skull, which had worked loose. To make sure he had received the correct message I now put a little more pressure on the screwdriver to cause a little pain. I was not wrong. He got the message. He winced.

I now took his head into my hands and shook it again.

'Not quite tight enough,' I said.

I turned it a few more times, until he winced again. I stopped. I shook his head again.

'That is much better,' I said and instructed him to come back every three months to have the screw tightened.

He had hardly moved during the whole operation except to wince when I had placed some extra pressure on the screwdriver. He had never been the brightest of persons. Conversation had always been difficult, and the lack of conversation in a situation such as this was not unusual. The only topic of conversation had always been his grating; now that I claimed to have cured it he was lost for words.

I explained that he was one of those rare people who required the screwdriver treatment and he would almost certainly never meet anybody with the same problem. In all my experience I had never previously met a case. It was lucky that I read the New England Journal of Medicine, a surgeon in Memphis had written about a case such as his and advised the treatment. He was a lucky chap that he had come on that day, and the treatment was still fresh in my mind.

I looked at him anxiously, waiting for him to say that my treatment had not worked, that I was a fake, that I was playing games. He just sat there uncomplaining, glued to his seat, staring at me.

He tried his head.

His eyes lit up. 'You've cured it! I've always told my friends you're bloody good!'

With those few remarks he left me, only to return regularly every three months for five long years to have the screw tightened. Whenever I cleaned out my desk after our first success I made sure the screwdriver remained in the drawer. I bought another one for home use.

On his last visit to me in 1980 he told me that he was leaving London to live in Birmingham and it was too far for him to return for treatment. I told him to be explicit with my instructions to his new doctor; the doctor would understand. He should tell him that he had a screw loose in his head, in the parietal area.

After hearing my diagnosis, I only hoped the doctor would have a steady hand and the right size screwdriver, to tighten the loose screw.

It was half past four in the afternoon on an unusually mild day in January 1970 when Sidney, a young six foot two inch Jamaican lad whom I had treated on many occasions previously, suddenly decided to go berserk and smash his way into the surgery. There was no explanation for the violence. The surgery doors were open. There was no reason why he had to use brute force to see me. He flung open the front door - there was no handle on this door - and finding the door between the waiting room and reception closed, smashed his way through it. This door was half-glazed, so the noise of shattering glass muffled a good deal of his shouting as he propelled himself into the receptionists' room.

Surgery consultations had already commenced so I left my room to see what all the commotion was about. I was confronted by an excited Sidney, towering over me, demanding my presence in accompanying him to have tea with the Queen at Buckingham Palace. His violent behaviour was quite uncharacteristic. He had always been a gentle giant and his manners had been impeccable. He worked in a printing establishment, had also been doing a secretarial course at evening classes, and we had already developed a friendly relationship. At that moment, these particulars were not the most important facts to occupy my thoughts.

I looked at him in astonishment as he shouted to me over and over again that I should accompany him to Buckingham Palace. I realised immediately that he had become acutely mentally disturbed. No one in Peckham goes to tea with the Queen without a written invitation!

Patients were already in the waiting room. If one is only five foot six and a half inches tall and not in the best physical condition, one does not - if one is sensible - argue with a chap who is over six feet tall, younger, more muscular, much fitter and not in command of his mental state. I was also not in the best position to resist. He had me in a headlock and was dragging me to the front door.

I tried to humour him. He was shouting at the top of his voice and in the commotion I was being forced to shout back at him. He would not have heard me otherwise. He kept repeating that a taxi be called to take us to the palace and I kept answering that - in the circumstances - it would be quicker if we used my car. After all, I shouted, we should not keep her Majesty waiting! I was told afterwards that patients who had already arrived for the evening surgery and were sitting in the waiting room had decided their ailments could wait for a more propitious occasion. They made a very quick, quiet, exit through the front door.

When Sidney had managed to negotiate me through the front door he saw my car and almost deafened me by shouting that I was right. We should go in my car, not be disrespectful to her Majesty.

As we got into the car I made up my mind not to take any chances with a maniac so I decided to drive as requested. I must admit however it was distracting - to say the least - to have a passenger singing ' God save the Queen' over and over again at the top of his voice, deafening me.

When we came to a red light I was thankful that he did not order me to ignore it! The light appeared to motivate him to sing louder. Drivers of cars, who had the misfortune of being alongside, gave us a quick look and tactfully turned away. They obviously could not tell which one of us had become so patriotic as to lose his marbles!

I was terrified. Mental patients do behave abnormally. I wondered how the situation would resolve itself. I still however had the presence of mind to drive along Walworth Road to the Elephant and Castle, double back through the back streets of Camberwell to Denmark Hill, then to De Crespigny Park. He sang the whole way and by doing so I knew my ruse of driving through the back doubles had fooled him; he had not doubted my sincerity in taking him to the Palace. The side entrance of the Institute of Psychiatry of Maudsley Hospital was in De Crespigny Park at that time. I was banking on the fact that he did not know this. I was right!

I was hoping that when I had deposited him outside the Maudsley Hospital he would believe, as it was now dark, it was the Palace. He would get out of the car quickly and allow me to make a quick get-away. This was not to be. He insisted that I get out first and still holding on to me slid out over the driving seat. When we both reached the pavement he changed his hold. He grabbed me once again around the neck, not to hurt me, but to drag me along with him. It was a painful experience being dragged by a maniac; the force he was using for my compliance was excessive. I nursed a bruised neck for several days afterwards.

With his arm around my neck, shouting to bystanders that we were going to have tea with the Queen, we walked - rather he walked and I was pushed - into the side entrance of the Maudsley Hospital. The few people who looked at us entering the hospital must have thought to themselves that those two are going into the right place. They kept well away.

I had been into the Maudsley Hospital on only one occasion. This was to take Mr Ward to the emergency clinic and the entrance had been the main one in Denmark Hill, opposite King's College Hospital. I did not know my way through the De Crespigny Park entrance. I was lost! I had however by this time ceased to care.

There was a flight of stairs immediately facing us at the entrance and since no one appeared to direct us to her Majesty Sidney decided that she must be waiting for us upstairs. We went up the stairs. All the way up he kept singing the National Anthem at the top of his voice. People in white coats kept coming out of side rooms telling us to be quiet. They made no effort to rescue me or find out the cause of the commotion. They could see that only one of us was so patriotic as to make his voice heard, but all they did was to look and shout, 'Please be quiet!'

We had reached the third floor of the building when he suddenly turned and dragged me through some swing doors. We now found ourselves in a large waiting room. I do not remember the department we were in except that we were in the Maudsley Hospital. I had chosen the hospital. He had chosen the department. In my plight this was good enough for me.

This waiting room however worried me; it was in urgent need of redecoration, not at all resembling a room at a palace. I had to find an excuse quickly; he still had his arm around my neck! I told him that this was not the room the Queen used for guests. This was obviously the booking-in room. Guests had to wait here until the Queen sent for them. There were chairs around the room for visitors. He could see that they were at present unoccupied. We were lucky! To prove my point I directed his intention to the other end of the room where a middle-aged lady receptionist sat behind a desk. She appeared to be taking no notice of us. Either she was used to this behaviour or was hoping that we were intending to make our presence felt in another department and were just passing through.

I managed to persuade Sidney to lower his voice as we were in the reception area of Buckingham Palace. We were obviously expected, the lady in reception had taken no notice of us. She knew who we were. She was only waiting for a message from the Queen to grant us an audience. Patience, patience was the order of the day. He should remember it was the Queen we were seeing and she was a very busy lady.

In a hushed voice, I whispered into his ear that travelling in the car through the streets of South London had dirtied my face and disturbed my hair. It was not right or proper to appear before her Majesty without a wash. I had to have a wash and intended to go to the washroom to make myself presentable. To my surprise he released me. To my amazement, as

I slowly walked to the toilet to avoid suspicion, he stretched himself full length on the floor and stopped singing 'God Save the Queen'. He thundered out 'Land of Hope and Glory' at the top of his voice instead. His voice was deep bass. This turn of events not only startled me, but the receptionist too. She stood up speechless and open mouthed, looked at me standing shell-shocked at the entrance to the washroom, then at Sidney on the floor.

I recovered quickly. I didn't bother to explain my predicament to the receptionist nor did I bother to ask Sidney the reason for the change in his singing, I fled! It would have taken too long to wait to explain the position to a hospital doctor had I remained. Besides, I knew that I had a heavy evening's work ahead of me at the surgery. I had left my patient to be cared for in a most fitting place - The Institute of Psychiatry - a prestigious, postgraduate, psychiatric teaching hospital.

Instead of going to the toilets, as he thought, I hurtled down the stairs to my car. I fled to the surgery and have never come down three flights of stairs so quickly in my life! Not surprisingly, I arrived back in a state of extreme agitation, exhausted both physically and mentally, apprehensive at what Sidney's move might be. His behaviour had been uncharacteristically bizarre. He was normally a docile creature. He would never have put a headlock on me had he not flipped. He would probably in his present confusion not discover my absence for some time. When however he did what would his reaction be? What would he then do? His mind had let him down. Mine was in a whirl! To be perfectly honest, I was terrified! There was a waiting room full of patients needing my services when I arrived back. I had no choice but to recommence doing, or pretending to do, a normal evening surgery.

An hour later the inevitable happened. A telephone call from a doctor in the Maudsley Hospital informed me that a patient of mine was causing a commotion in the reception area of the neurosurgical unit. He was lying stretched out on the floor singing 'God Save the Queen', at the top of his voice. Sidney had switched tunes again. When questioned, he insisted that he was a patient of Dr Crown of Bellenden Road, and was just waiting for him to reappear, as they were waiting to be called to have tea with the Queen. He was adamant. Dr Crown had definitely been with him when he had come into the building and had just gone to make himself presentable. The receptionist had corroborated his statement that he had been accompanied by a man when he came into reception but could not be certain who the other fellow was. Sidney had the poor fellow in a headlock when they first appeared and when he let him go she had only a fleeting view of his face. She thought at first the fellow in the headlock was a patient, therefore did not pay much attention until Sidney had laid himself on the floor.

'Have tea with the Queen? I don't know what you are talking about.' I pretended to be dumbfounded. 'The man must be mad. A fellow from Peckham who believes that he can have tea with the Queen just by turning up in your hospital should be admitted! I would send him down to the emergency clinic if I were you and see what they say about him. Incidentally, I would be extremely grateful if you would tell me what you have done with him. If he is a patient of mine I don't want to be called out in the middle of the night to a raving lunatic.'

This doctor with his clipped South African accent was real nice fellow. He telephoned me later to tell me that the fellow in reception was a psychopath. When asked by the receptionist to stop singing he had gone berserk. He had broken every chair in reception in his fury, smashed the desk, and attacked the nurses who had come to remove him. The police had been called; a straitjacket had been used to restrain him. He had been admitted for treatment under a 'police section'.

Some years later, when I was shopping in Rye Lane, a tall young Jamaican lad tapped me on the shoulder. I turned around. It was Sidney. He had recognised me and was beaming like a long lost friend. He told me that as his family had moved to Deptford and as his new address was out of my practice area his family had changed his doctor. I made no mention of our last meeting or whether he was having any treatment. He appeared to be completely normal and we parted the best of friends.

Another patient who went berserk without warning was Lionel Nash who went berserk in 1961. He broke into the local liberal club in Elm Grove one evening after the club was closed and smashed all the bottles on the shelves. He made no attempt to escape from the scene of the crime. The police who were called were startled to find him sitting at the bar quite sober, chuckling, and gurgling over his performance. The police had no alternative except to arrest him as he had committed a crime but were reluctant to charge him as his behaviour was so out of the ordinary. The magistrate, before whom he appeared on the following day, refused to pass sentence until he received a psychiatric report. He was examined by a doctor at the Maudsley Hospital who decided that Lionel was mentally disturbed and should be admitted under a police section. Unfortunately, another doctor saw him after a few days' treatment, disagreed with the first doctor's findings, and sent our Lionel home with tablets and an outpatient appointment.

Doctors in the past tended to be very insular, dogmatic, and frequently disagreed over diagnoses and treatment. Indeed, they have been known to dislike one another so intensely over different methods of treatment as to come to blows. I have always liked the cartoon that showed a patient on a bed with his hair standing on end and a doctor on each side of his bed quarrelling. One doctor is saying to the other, 'You see if I am not right at the post mortem!'

Lionel was fine for two weeks until he attended hospital again. He saw another doctor who disagreed with the other two doctors' findings and stopped all medication.

That night, Lionel celebrated by breaking all the show windows of Jones and Higgins - the largest store in Peckham - and once again the police found him at the seat of the crime, gloating, and making no attempt to escape capture. One of the policemen at the station recognised him, did not make an arrest, but took him back again to hospital for treatment.

He was admitted, kept in hospital for seven days, then discharged back to my care. The letter I received advised treatment but no further outpatient appointments. Faced with the situation that the hospital wanted riddance of this nuisance and not being psychiatrically orientated I wondered how I was going to cope with this man. I had already spent more of my time than I could reasonably afford in dealing with Lionel, but as Lionel was only 25 years old, and as he had employment as a low-grade council worker, I decided to make every effort to keep him at work.

I already knew that Lionel would discontinue his medication immediately his present supply had run out. I wracked my brain for a solution. It occurred to me that if I found a physical cause for medication he would - being of low intelligence - continue taking the drugs even though he complained they caused him to feel sleepy. I told him he had a hernia! This would require continuous medication; otherwise he would suffer intolerable pain and end up on the operating table. If he took my advice he would avoid the surgeon's knife.

He was a model patient and was monitored by me every eight weeks for thirty years for his hernia. He then came in a little early asking my advice. His father had died four days earlier at home, without any medical advice being requested, and he wanted to know what to do with the body. No doctor had seen his father for over twenty years and his mother was now being disturbed at having to sleep in another room! We settled this matter to everyone's satisfaction as I reported the problem to the coroner. I have heard since leaving the National Health Service that he developed diabetes, has departed this life, and has no longer any need to take his medication.

To Thailand For Love

Harold was old and ugly. He looked every bit of his seventy-two years. He had a scar the whole length of the left side of his face. He also sported an ugly-looking deaf aid.

I had occasion to see him in my surgery only a couple of times as he was not a National Health patient of mine. He worked for a firm of bookmakers in the New Cross Road and, as he did not live locally, I agreed to see him when the occasion arose as a friendly gesture to his employer, Dave Moss, who was at that time the warden of the local synagogue.

I learned from Dave Moss that Harry was a bachelor. He lived alone and his whole life centred on travelling to Bangkok twice a year on holiday. Bangkok, in the late `sixties and early `seventies was not quite on the beaten track, certainly not in the cheap travel brochures. Only the truly wealthy could afford to make the trip. It would have needed a bachelor to save up his pay for six months to be able to do so.

A few weeks after I first met him in my surgery, he turned up in the South East London Synagogue, New Cross Road, on the Day of Atonement. Yom Kippur, the most holy day in the Jewish calendar, is a long day of prayer and fasting. The morning service commences at 8.30 a.m. or thereabouts and services continue non-stop throughout the day until sunset, when the fast ends. There is therefore ample time during the day - for the not so prayer minded - to hold conversations with their neighbours.

Harry, to his credit, remained all day. He could not read Hebrew well and must have found the services extremely tedious. During that first Yom Kippur afternoon in 1968 he made friends with my sons who were sitting next to him and proceeded to show them photographs of Thailand.

I was sitting in the row immediately in front of them and my sons took it upon themselves to interrupt their father's prayers to show me these photographs. They were enjoying themselves, having a break from praying, even though they could not be accused of playing. Most of the photographs he had taken himself. Included in the views were several of a beautiful Thai girl. He told them that she was his girlfriend.

She looked as though she was in her twenties and the photographs included pictures of her children. They were most certainly not his; their appearance was that of native Thais. Among the photographs were pictures of her parents and their village in the north of Thailand. He had not as yet visited the parents in their village as it was a long way from Bangkok. He was saving up. He hoped to be able to do so on his next trip.

There was one photograph that was missing - that of his girlfriend's husband. He was quite happy to admit that she had one. It did not appear to disturb him. He had no intention of marrying the girl, just befriending her. He had met his girlfriend in Bangkok in a bar. She had been working there as a hostess and the snide remarks of people when he told them this did not seem to offend or embarrass him in any way.

I saw him again the following year - he never attended synagogue except on Yom Kippur - and in that year the girl's family had grown. This had meant extra presents. He now had to include her sister and the sister's husband amongst the recipients of his beneficence and arrangements had been made by his girlfriend for him to see them on his next visit to Bangkok. He then produced more photographs of Thailand including the parents' village where he had spent a weekend. In the photographs the village looked gorgeous but his description of his visit there gave a different slant to the pictures.

The parents lived in a hut on stilts, over a lake, with no proper sanitation. The waste matter - including that of the toilet - disappeared into the lake. He was forced to admit that he was glad to get back to his hotel after a weekend there. The hut stank. The village stank. The food was diabolical. He had not been able to eat any of their cooked food and had lived on a diet of fresh fruit. He had suffered from diarrhoea. The only redeeming feature of his visit was the friendliness of the people. Their genuine hospitality had made the smells somewhat bearable.

He returned to the synagogue the following year with yet more fascinating stories of his visit to Thailand. I felt very sorry for him as he appeared to have no social life between these visits and to have no friends in London. I never heard him speak of any family whether alive or dead. It seemed from the conversations I had with him that the only affection he had ever received in his whole life was from this girl. She and her family were obviously giving him love for the financial benefits they obtained. His belief in their sincerity was such that I would never have said anything to destroy it.

In the fourth year he never returned to the synagogue so I asked Dave Moss where he was.

'Silly old fool went to Bangkok in June and dropped down dead on the dance floor,' he answered.

Dr Blank

Doctor Blank (Merton), had been a practising single-handed general practitioner in Choumert Road, Peckham, before becoming one of the founder members of our Group Practice in Bellenden Road in 1967. He had first come down to London from Southport to succeed Dr McKay who had a surgery in Choumert Road. Poor Dr McKay had died whilst attending a patient; I was informed at the time that the patient had been annoyed at not having received a sick note absenting him from work before the arrival of the *grim reaper*.

Merton was a loveable eccentric. He was blunt to the extreme. An impish man with an infectious laugh. Many of his eccentricities could perhaps have been laid at the door of the conditions of his upbringing. His parents had been very poor. This would help to explain the fact that he would go to extraordinary lengths to save money. He could not get used to the habit of spending money, even when he eventually had some and could afford to spend it.

Medicine was not his first career. He was an industrial chemist having obtained a first class honours degree from Manchester University. His work took him to Paris for a year or so and while there he took the opportunity to learn to speak French. Unfortunately, when he returned to this country, his employers put him on the night shift - without consultation. He handed in his notice. On failing to secure new employment after six months he went back to Manchester University for advice; it was at their suggestion that he took up a medical career.

He was very bright fellow. He qualified easily. He was an excellent diagnostician. His only failing was that he lacked bedside manner. Many patients were terrified of him. Patients had to be genuinely ill before Dr Blank would be civil to them. It became a joke in the practice that if a patient was given a certificate to stay away from work he was probably at death's door!

His economical behaviour, although frequently commented on both by patients and staff, was not exclusively devoted to the work place - it was even more stringently applied at home. Merton's wife, Lena, used to say to the children, 'You tell me what you want and I will tell you how to manage without it!'

She knew that unless the article was essential Merton would not countenance its purchase. She had experience of his behaviour from the time they first met. She lost the use of her car - Merton appropriated it. Eventually, her driving licence expired: she was forced to use buses to do her shopping and visit her friends.

Merton made two stipulations when he bought a new car. His new car had to have a starting handle. He used to crank up the engine of his car every morning, to save the battery! The second condition was that the car did not have an automatic choke as this would lead to a slight wastage of petrol. He would never have been happy with a modern car!

When his son learned to drive Merton sold him his car second hand, at what his son believed to be the second-hand market price. When his son traded it in for a new one, after passing the driving test, he found his father had overcharged him for it! The cost of running a car has always been an expensive item. However, Merton of necessity having to own one by virtue of his work, devised many economies. When he wanted to signal he declined to use the indicators - prior to that the trafficators - because at some point he would have to replace a bulb. Instead, he would wind down the window and give hand signals. It might be snowing, the passengers shivering from cold from the open window, it made not a scrap of difference.

Whenever he did some gardening, or cleaned the car, he would never use a belt to hold up his trousers; he made do with an old tie. After cleaning the car he would enter the house and get hold of a member of the family help push it back into the garage. He would never dream of starting it by using the starter motor - this would have led to some drain on the battery.

He was never seen to use a handkerchief. He always used tissues, usually those that came with a box of apples. He would polish his shoes after every wear; by this means he managed to make them last indefinitely. When his shoelaces broke, rather than buy new ones, he made do by tying the broken ends.

One of the many economies his family were made to suffer was not to use more than two inches of water in the bath. Even today, when his son Henry manages to indulge himself in a bath half full of water, he is left with a feeling of guilt. The little hair he had he always washed with soap. He mocked people who went to the spendthrift extreme of using shampoo. He was meticulous in dental care, but instead of buying toothpicks used his penknife to whittle down old matches.

His son was made to keep a log of his telephone calls and to pay for them when the quarterly bill arrived. When one day he telephoned the surgery to speak to his father Merton was heard to say, 'Where are you speaking from? ....My house? ....Get off the phone! I will speak to you later.'

He would not wear socks, whatever the weather. Many are the stories told to me by patients who knew of this peculiarity. At one committee meeting of the St. Mary's Road General Practitioners' Centre, I was met by the acid remarks of Dr Moss, one of the members. 'Your group practice, Dr Crown, must be in severe financial trouble if you can't afford to pay your partner enough to buy himself a pair of socks!' This of course was followed by shrieks of laughter at my expense. I was really not embarrassed. All the doctors on the committee knew of his behaviour. Patients would take great delight in telling me that they had seen Dr Blank walking in Ruskin Park, Denmark hill, whatever the weather. He was reading a newspaper, wearing torn trousers and slippers, and without a hat or coat.

One day, just as I was about to commence an evening surgery, a patient whom I knew very well rushed into my surgery to tell me that he had just seen a poofter, changing his trousers, in a car near the surgery. It was at the corner outside the Albert Public House. He was amused and wanted me to join in the fun.

'It shouldn't be allowed. You should report it,' he said.

I went with him to see the remarkable event. I was terribly disappointed. It was just Merton changing into smart trousers, that he wore when doing a surgery, from the threadbare ones which he wore when driving his car.

He was just being economical!

The staff of the surgery loved, understood, and had a great affection for him. They looked forward each day to another Dr Blank episode. He had this great ability, which is extremely rare, of being able to laugh at himself. He would throw his head back, laugh uproariously, even though he himself might be the victim - the object of the merriment. One of their many pranks, knowing his love of sweets, was to offer him a sweet. He never refused, and they would leave the remainder in a bag on a desk. When he thought no one was looking, with his back to the desk, he would thrust his hand into the bag and take some more. Someone would then go to take a sweet and remark, 'some *thieving rat bag* has taken more than his fair share!'

At a postgraduate lecture at the General Practitioners' Centre, one Thursday afternoon, the sister in charge of the centre called me out of the room to have a quiet word with me. She was silent for some time, and I could see that she did not know how to approach the subject.

'Do you know that your partner, Dr Blank, takes biscuits during the tea interval, hides them in his pocket like a naughty boy, then eats them in the toilet?' she said.

She told me the story in a loud whisper, for my ears only; not to be heard even by the walls. She was so embarrassed. As she concluded her recital I fell about laughing, and her attitude changed completely. She realised it was nothing which gave me concern or that would cause disharmony in our group practice by her disclosure. She was not in any way going to be the cause of a break up of the group. In between peals of laughter I promised to buy her packets of biscuits to replace the loss. When she saw my reaction she could not contain herself. She saw the funny side of her story and she too burst into peals of laughter. She told me that she had never come across a situation like this before. In between laughter I told her that neither had I!

Dr Blank's relationship with Nellie, the housekeeper who lived on the practice premises, gave us in the practice many a chuckle. Merton was an orthodox Jew. Although he would do a consulting surgery on Friday evening in the winter when the Sabbath had already commenced, he would not switch lights on and off. He would shout, 'NELLIE! *Shabbos!* Lights!'

She would shuffle down the garden where his surgery was situated to do his bidding.

When the garden gate broke down he would shout, 'NELLIE! Gate!' Once again she would appear; this time with hammer and nails.

She grew fruit in the garden. He waited until they became ripe and when her back was turned he stole them. It was a game they played. The only remark from her when she noticed the loss when she came to pick her fruit was, 'that thieving rat bag has pinched my fruit again!'

His obsession with cost cutting had no limits. This passion for saving money brought him into conflict with me, and the other doctors, on many occasions. He was so keen to save money in the surgery that he would switch off the electric light and fire in my consulting room the minute I left it, even if I intended to return. He would accept my explanation that his action was not cost-effective; fluorescent lights were better left on, rather than switched on and off incessantly. This did not deter him. Old habits die hard. He continued to switch my lights and fire off!

We had many a tussle over his behaviour, perhaps he over mine, but we always parted the best of friends. There was no way anyone could make an enemy of this man. I must admit I was fond of him. He was a character, but a loveable one. Although he had the name of being mean and miserly he was the most liberal host when I was a guest in his home.

I had the privilege of being his general practitioner. And I was very saddened when the heart trouble - which had shortened his work pattern in the latter years - finally ended his life at much too early an age.

Dr Cook Enjoyed Psychiatric Work

Dr Cook, one of my partners in the practice for over twenty years, spent most of his time treating mentally ill patients. His interest was psychiatry, as psychiatric patients behave abnormally we had problems on dozens of occasions. Some of the experiences were frightening as many of his patients were psychotic. Many threatened suicide; some even carried out their threats. Our good fortune was that no one actually carried out his or her threat on our premises!

One confused lady patient of his always came to the surgery to see him in a different garb. I did not know the lady. On the first occasion I had the good fortune to see her enter the premises I was very respectful, I raised my hat. I opened the door to let the 'nun' pass through. On the second occasion however, a week later, I was in a state of shock: the same lady appeared in the bizarre habit of a fortune-teller. I learned that her real profession was dipsomania. It should have been pyromania for she ended her life by setting fire to herself.

Another patient of his, an ex-nurse, always came to the surgery with a basketful of apple pies. She baked them especially for him. The receptionists in the surgery never refused her an appointment and always looked forward to her attendances. She was an excellent baker and Dr Cook always passed these pies around. They were very much enjoyed. One day however she decided that her pies were much too good for this world and took them with her into the next!

Dr Cook loved to visit his weird patients and had a rapport with them. He spent hours chatting with what he called his nuts.

One of his nuts, Albert, in his fifties, hated women. He tolerated his mother and sister visiting him only because they cared for his daily needs. He had not worked for years and had turned his flat into a 'cesspit'. When his family found it was no longer possible to care properly for him, they turned to Dr Cook for help.

Albert had always treated Dr Cook as a friend and had always allowed him access to his flat without protest. Now this friendship was going to be put to the test. Albert's family had asked Dr Cook to arrange for Albert to be admitted to a psychiatric institution in whatever way he thought best. Whether it was to be as a voluntary patient, or compulsorily, was going to be for Dr Cook to decide. They could not take the disturbance to their lives any more. Albert had decided to play his old '78' gramophone records at full volume all day. They were deafened, the other occupants of the house were deafened and so were the neighbours. He had become a public nuisance. The neighbours had called the police.

Dr Cook went to see him and, as his friend, persuaded him to go into the Maudsley Hospital as a voluntary patient. After all the arrangements for his admission had been made Albert suddenly asked Dr Cook whether, before going into hospital, he could telephone the Queen to tell her what had taken place. This turn of events took the learned doctor by surprise but he had no alternative except to agree. After all, Albert had agreed to be admitted into a psychiatric hospital as a voluntary patient!

Albert disappeared into the next room to telephone the Queen and was away for what appeared to his family to be hours. He then returned to inform Dr Cook that he had had great difficulty in getting through to her Majesty. Every obstacle had been put in his way by the palace staff to prevent him speaking to her. He was not to be put off. He had finally managed to speak to the Queen and asked her whether she wanted him to go into hospital. She told him there was no point in him going into hospital as there was nothing wrong with him. She did not want him to go. As her loyal subject he had to respect her wishes.

Even though Dr Cook knew that Albert had not spoken to the queen he did not wish to antagonise a mental patient. His answer to Albert was that he would have to defer his admission to hospital as he did not want to end up in the Tower!

Early Days Proved Unusual

I began to practise as a single-handed General Practitioner in Peckham on the 12th of January 1953, and on the thirteenth of May in the year 2000 I was granted the Honorary Liberty of Camberwell, by the Borough of Southwark, for my long service in the practice.

It had been a battle to get the practice in the first place for all my applications for vacancies in London had previously been rejected. The excuse given on every occasion was lack of experience. The army service with married families in my posting in Germany appeared to be of no value when I went for interview at a vacancy. A panel of laypersons conducted interviews for vacancies and at a vacancy for a practice in Acton one of the members, when he learned that I had done my army service in Neumünster, in Germany, asked me how much tropical medicine I had practised! At that period we had a surplus of general practitioners. The NHS was in its infancy and as so many doctors had been demobilised after the war had ended my services were apparently not required.

The house, which we moved into in Bellenden Road, was fitted out as best as we could. It was the middle one of a terrace of three houses and there was a small front garden that we later used as a car park. We used the two downstairs rooms for practice use and the kitchen as well as upstairs rooms for living accommodation. The large back garden was very useful in later years as we were able to build surgeries in it when the practice was large enough to become a Group Practice.

My first patient was not long in coming. Mr William Godley came exactly two hours after the removal van had left. I examined him by candlelight as electricity had not yet been connected because the roof leaked and water had affected the wiring. We also had no telephone. Even though a doctor was regarded as a priority for phone connection, we still had to wait four days.

I had inherited the practice from Dr Morgan, an elderly GP in his eighties. He had died whilst still working, but his inheritance to me of NHS patients was exactly two hundred. This number was a very small nucleus to work on to make a satisfactory living for a young married doctor with a small son. Fortunately conditions in the area however were in my favour. The London Executive Council had correctly determined that the district needed a young enthusiastic doctor. My list of patients increased every week.

Finances were my main problem so to make ends meet I worked as a locum doing night visits for ten doctors in the East End of London, for two pounds a night.

My practice grew so rapidly - I worked a 24 hour day seven days a week schedule - that by 1955 I had already built up enough goodwill to allow me to employ a regular locum for Saturday mornings. This not only gave me some rest from the workshop but also allowed me to attend Sabbath morning services in the local synagogue in New Cross and to spend some time with my son. The Saturday locums were not general practice trained but - as at that time a doctor by his arrangement with the authorities had to be available at all times - these doctors provided a useful purpose in attending to emergencies.

Locums and assistants were always a problem. In 1963 - exactly ten years after I had commenced my career - I had over 3500 patients. For one doctor to be responsible for so many people was just too much. I took a partner, Dr Leslaw Kwasny. A more pleasant man it would be hard to find. He was conscientious, friendly and an excellent diagnostician. The problem with our relationship was, although the practice still increased in numbers it did not increase rapidly enough in two years to satisfy him. He applied for a vacant practice in Dulwich. On being successful, he wanted us to combine practices. His practice had two surgeries, one in Barry Road and the other in Woodwarde Road. This would have entailed us in doing six surgeries a day. I still shudder at the thought. He accepted the vacant practice as a single-handed practitioner but we remained the best of friends.

I sought a replacement doctor and Dr Faridian, a young Persian doctor, agreed terms with me to accept an assistantship with a view to partnership, after six months mutual assessment. This fellow was every girl's dream of what a young doctor should be like. He was tall, dark, olive skinned, handsome and debonair with a face that carried a perpetual smile. He commenced four weeks before Christmas in 1965 and in four weeks he had charmed me, my wife and every patient he had treated. There was no doubt in my mind that he was someone who was going to be easy to work with and make an ideal partner. I therefore intended to wait until after the holiday and offer him an immediate share in the practice.

I had, until that year, always been on duty over the Christmas period. However, on his insistence, as he was not a Christian, he wanted to be on duty that Christmas and take the Persian New Year as a holiday instead. We therefore arranged that he would be on duty and I would go to visit my mother in Liverpool and return on the day after Boxing Day. As I would not be returning early on December 27th, it was arranged that he would do the morning consultation surgery on his own. Divine providence instructed me not to allow an assistant to be on his own on a busy morning after the holiday period! In spite of the elements - it snowed all the time we were in Liverpool and all the way back to London - I returned with my family in the early hours of the morning of December 27th after a nine hour car journey. It has to be remembered that there was no motorway at that time. I was exhausted.

At 10.15 a.m. the telephone rang. The housekeeper at the surgery was hysterical. She was being pestered by a waiting room full of patients demanding to know when the doctor intended to appear. I was dumbfounded. I telephoned Dr Faridian and there was no reply. There was no alternative. I dressed, went to Bellenden Road and did the surgery myself.

I telephoned the doctor several times a day for two weeks to contact him - with no success. He lived in Battersea so I sent him a registered letter and as it was not returned I naturally assumed that he had received it. After working single-handed for three months, I received a call from my charming absentee attempting to explain his absence from my surgery. He had been in an Ear Nose and Throat Hospital and would come to see me to explain his absence. I had not bothered to ask whether his presence in the hospital was that of an employee or patient! I am still waiting for him to call.

When reading a newspaper some years later my eyes riveted on a photograph - it was my friend who had deserted me for pastures new. He had a practice in Battersea and was being accused by a patient of making amorous advances. He was evidently acquitted; so much time has elapsed I cannot remember the details. A patient of mine saw this photograph and I then learned the reason why he had left my practice in such a hurry.

After I had left for Liverpool on that evening before Christmas 1965 he received a call to visit a patient whom he did not know was on my medical list. It was to a young child and he knew who the boy was. It was his son. The mother had been a nurse in the hospital where Dr Faridian had qualified and they had been lovers. He must have been absolutely shocked to find that he intended to become a partner in a practice where his wild oats would perpetually haunt him. Single mothers were very much frowned upon in those days. He obviously had no intention of marrying the mother.

In the same circumstances perhaps I would have behaved in the same fashion!

Criminal Became A Freemason

An old patient of mine called Wilfred Roberts, known as Fred, was born in Peckham, on 18.12.43. He can be called a real Peckhamite for he has lived in the area - apart from being held in institutions at Her Majesty's pleasure - all his life. He describes himself as being a rough diamond and from my experience his description is one hundred per cent accurate. He has never failed to help when called at any time of the day or night. As he relates the story of his life it is surprising that he has developed into the type of man he now is.

His father died in 1951 and he remembers seeing him only two days before his death. He believes he died of tuberculosis contracted whilst he was working in the Home Guard and digging people out of bombed houses after the air raids in the 1939-45 war. His father had been ill for several years before his demise, unable to work, and Fred's mother had been forced to be the breadwinner for the large family.

His only memory of his father was being called to his bedroom in Parkstone Road, with his brother Alfie. The bedroom was bare except for lino on the floor. His father was in bed, breathing with difficulty, and he gave Fred a red fire engine and a half crown. He never saw his father again!

The terraced house in which they lived in Parkstone Road was on two floors with an outside toilet. There was also a small garden at the back, this was just large enough for his father to keep a few chickens and a mongrel dog called Pongo.

There was an old tin bath in the garden which, when the necessity arose for the children to bathe, was filled with water which the mother had heated up in the scullery on an old copper coal-fed boiler. The boys slept in the back upstairs bedroom, in one bed. As there were four children to be accommodated, two slept at one end of the bed and two at the other end.

Next door lived the large French family. The family name was French not the nationality; incidentally, this family were also patients of mine. When the parents of this family fought, the whole street could hear the commotion. The f...ing and blinding continued until Mr French left the family residence and made his way to the pub. He was a radio engineer and was the only person in the street to own a small television set with a large magnifying glass in front of it.

Parkstone Road is off Rye Lane in Peckham, and nearby at that period was the Tower Cinema. This was one of the best cinemas in London with marble stairs, brass handrails and a foyer with a rising cinema organ. Fred and his friends went to this cinema regularly. One of his friends would pay at the desk in the foyer and enter the cinema. He would then open the fire emergency exit doors and the others would quickly enter the cinema in this way, without troubling the girl in the foyer! This ruse was not always successful. When they were caught they were given a clip around the ear and thrown out. They were never prosecuted. He now muses that such behaviour by the cinema attendants at this time would allow him to sue for assault!

Fred was a tearaway. His best friend was Siddy Rivers, who lived only a few doors away, in the same street. Mr Rivers, his friend's father, was a French Polisher. He earned good money; Sidney could wear nice clothes and have toys that Fred's mother could never hope to provide for her family.

One evening, as they were roaming the streets, they decided to go on to the railway embankment. This was not an unusual experience as they often went down Rye Lane, through the gates of the C & A store, into the railway arches to the shunting yard and start up a coal lorry for fun. They would attempt to drive the lorry; more often than not they damaged the back of a lorry by attempting to back it into a space in the yard. On this particular evening they climbed up the metal rail ladders to the railway line but failed to cross the railway lines as they normally did. Siddy slipped on the dead line and fell between it and the live line. Fred ran back to him. Siddy looked as if he was on fire. He was covered in smoke and there was a smell of burning flesh. Fred knew that he was unable to help so ran to the Stationmaster who immediately cut off the electricity supply. Siddy was taken to hospital and it was many weeks before Fred saw him again. He had suffered severe burns on his face and one side of his body. When Fred was finally allowed to visit him, Siddy still had skin grafts on his face that had not yet healed. Fred was grounded. He became lonely and depressed: in his childish mind he wondered, 'what life was about.'

Another of the friends' pranks was to go to with friends to Peckham Rye station on Sunday and buy one ticket to Fawkham, in Kent. Whenever they were asked to produce a ticket the holder of the ticket would show it, pass it surreptitiously to his friend on the train and it then went along the line of friends. One ticket would buy them a day out in the country away from Peckham. They would knock on farmers' doors asking for a drink of water knowing full well that the farmer would take pity on them and provide biscuits and lemonade.

They were not always lucky on their trips. One week they found a chicken farm with hen houses. Fred being the youngest, and small, climbed up the chicken-run ladder and made his way into the hen house. He passed out as many eggs as he could to his friends and they took the eggs home. When he tried the same escapade again on another occasion, on leaving the hen house with a shirt bulging with eggs, he saw his friend Paul speaking to a stranger on the path. He knew instinctively that this was the farmer so he threw the eggs into the bushes. Unfortunately, the farmer had seen him. Fred had been shouting to one of his friends and when the farmer found the eggs in the bushes he knew why his eggs had so frequently disappeared. He apprehended Paul and Fred and then called the police who caught the other two associates. They were taken to the police station and put in a cell. By then Fred's mother had remarried and the police sent someone to their home in Peckham to ask the stepfather collect the boys. He went to Kent and they were bailed to appear in court two weeks later. Fred's description of his return cannot be bettered. ' I was given the belt across my arse, with my trousers down, although he had quite a job trying to catch me. I would scream and shout as I tried to get out of the kitchen door.

'I never managed to escape. I was made aware at my first meeting with this man that my stepfather was Uncle John to me and not Dad. I believed that he hated me and I was terrified of him even though at times I obviously deserved chastisement.

'When my friends and I appeared at the magistrates court in Kent two weeks later we were remanded in custody for reports. Custody was in a detention centre for delinquent children, where the routine was strict and stern. This was so long ago my only memory of the place is that we made up our minds to escape at the first available opportunity.'

Two of the friends did escape one day by climbing through the roof. They were quickly caught, taken before the headmaster, and all privileges were stopped. They did not realise what the privileges were until the weekend when all the children were taken to the afternoon cinema. The two attempted escapees were physically pulled out of the queue of children, taken to an empty room at the top of the building and locked in. They spent the afternoon crying. Eventually they appeared in court and were allowed home on one year's probation. They had to report to the probation officer once a week for the first six months then once a month.

At this time Fred's mother was working as a cook, in the Reindeer public house, in Rye Lane, opposite the Tower Cinema. When the time was propitious she would provide his friends with food at the back door. By this means, the boys quickly learned the short cuts to the back doors of the shops in Rye Lane.

Sundays were now spent robbing the shops, or if the weather was favourable they went to the countryside on the train. Burglary was made possible by the fact that Fred was the smallest of the gang. He would climb the drainpipe and squeeze through the small toilet window. For some reason this window always appeared to be open. He would then walk down the staircase, to the fire exit, and let the other gang members in. They would hide behind the counters while they made their 'purchases'. They would often see a patrolling policeman pass by, give a cursory look in through the front of the shop, and pass on. As Fred related the story he said he believed every shop in Rye Lane was at one time or another visited by his gang. They were not stealing to make money they were just boys into mischief and to prove the point their favourite shops were sweet shops. Here they would have a ball! They would sit and eat sweets until they were sick. More often than not they would feel so ill through the amount they had consumed that they were not fit enough to take anything from the shop with them.

One Sunday they decided to rob Dolcis, a shoe shop in Rye Lane. This event is still fixed in his memory. They were, by this time, well known to the criminal fraternity who would buy their wares at knockdown prices - long before Del Boy in 'Only Fools and Horses' was born! They filled two dustbins with shoes and gleefully managed to drag them to one of the fences. They were repulsed with disgust! One of the fences said, 'You kids are not right in the head! All these shoes are for the right foot!'

One bonfire night they found a live cartridge. One of the boys held it in a pair of pliers, Fred put a nail in the detonator and struck it with a hammer. He will never do it again! The noise deafened him. The cartridge vanished and the pliers disappeared with it!

Some of the escapades involved churches and the Almighty in his wisdom made them pay for their wickedness. Myatts Park Church was frequently visited; they would climb the Bell Tower to steal pigeon eggs. On one occasion they found money left by worshippers after a service and took the money up with them into the Bell Tower. They were caught by the police, taken to the police station and charged with breaking and entering, wilful damage and theft. For this crime he was first given a good belting by Uncle John and then made to appear at Brixton Town Hall magistrates' court in the following week.

They were sentenced to two weeks in Stamford House in Hammersmith. This place was like a prison. There was barbed wire around the perimeter; doors were locked after you, and warders with jangling keys wandered through the building. For a boy just nine years old it was terrifying experience. The knowledge of being in this place has never left him. They were given food, but never ate it. They were too frightened to eat. They were in the place for two weeks. It felt like a lifetime!

They were taken back to the court after two weeks and put in the dock. Fred could just see above it; his friend, much smaller, could not. The magistrate was a short fat man with a beard and imposing figure. People with files in their hands were scurrying about. Several people were called to give a report on the boys and finally Uncle John was called. The magistrate then told the boys that as he had not yet received a report and they were uncontrollable they would be remanded for a further two weeks. They spent the two weeks crying the whole time.

When Fred reappeared before the magistrate he was sentenced to three years probation and warned of dire consequences should his behaviour not improve. His behaviour improved so much that he was expelled from Peckham Manor School for playing truant! He was transferred to William Penn School, in Adys Road, where it was hoped the discipline might cure his failure to attend. Unfortunately his truancy continued so he was asked to appear outside the headmaster's study for a lecture. Outside the study there were two other boys waiting as the headmaster had not yet appeared. Fred asked the boys to keep watch while he went into the study. On opening one of the drawers of the desk he found a wad of money. He took it out to show the boys. One of the boys refused to be a party to the theft but the other boy agreed to join him in the deed and they went to Battersea Fun Fair. They had the time of their lives.

When they arrived home that night the police were waiting at the house. The other friendly face was that of Uncle John, who was stroking his undone belt with his hands. After he had treated him with it he was taken to Peckham Police Station and charged with stealing money from the headmaster who was saving it for a school journey. The headmaster had been collecting money, weekly, from poor parents, so that their children would not be deprived of accompanying the other children at the yearly outing. At the time Fred did not know that there was to be a school journey for his parents were too poor to be in the scheme. Fred still has feelings of guilt over this event!

He was remanded in Stamford House and on appearing in court was sentenced to three years' probation. This allowed him to pursue his career of petty thieving. One of his accomplices persuaded him that Dulwich Baths was a good place to continue his education and he agreed by frequenting the area where the changing rooms were situated. Cubicles in swimming baths have gaps in the doors' top and bottom. Fred was small and thin so able to crawl under the doors. Rich pickings were his as he continued his unrelenting career. Unfortunately for him, on one of these operations, while crawling out from under the door of a cubicle, he was helped to his feet by the arms of the law. He was taken to Tower Bridge Magistrate's Court, remanded once again in Stamford House for reports and sentenced to 3 years in an Approved School - for uncontrollable behaviour. He was taken from the court to Stamford House where he remained for three weeks while a decision was made as to which school would be most suitable for his problem. Finally he was sent to Mile Oak Approved School in Portslade, Sussex.

He was absolutely devastated on the journey down to this school. He had done nothing wrong. He felt his world had come to an end. He had never physically hurt a soul, his reward had been to lose his freedom. Why was his mother not getting him out of this nightmare? He had only been walking the streets and making his own   entertainment. He was only eleven years old; why should he have to be so severely punished?

The school was a large country mansion, with marble floors. There were two other boys with him. A big fat man, who spoke with a click in his mouth, met them. His first words barked out to them were, 'Whenever your name is called out you will answer Sir!'

'Wilfred Roberts.'

'Sir.'

'I will call you Wilf from now on. Go along the corridor to the storeroom and pick up your bed linen and clothes.'

'Yes sir.'

He went along the corridor and was met in the room by a woman. She was ugly, with big buckteeth, but appeared friendly. Her greeting too was friendly.

'I am your housemother. I will meet you later with your housemaster and explain the routine of the house.'

She gave the boys blankets and clothes. They followed her to the bath area.

'You will take off your clothes, have a shower, then put on your school uniforms,' she said.

They went into an enormous room with a glass roof and a row of at least thirty basins. At the end of the room stood a shower unit with nine showers and an open window. They followed instructions. They took off their clothes, showered and put on the uniforms. The water was ice cold and they dressed as quickly as they could.

It was late November. It was freezing cold; they were in that room on their own, but not for long! As fast as they could they climbed through the open window - with a drop of about eight feet to the ground - on to an access road. This road led to a cornfield. It was pouring with rain; the rain lashed their faces. Added to the discomfort, the corn was so tall it whipped their heads as they raced through the field. They came to a courtyard with barns on either side and went into one of them. Then they climbed up one of the bales and snuggled up in the loose hay. Hours later they were awakened by the barking of a dog and the light of a torch in their faces. There was a shout. 'What the hell is this? Get up and come with me.'

They did as they were told. They followed the man to a caravan where a lady undressed them and dried their clothes. Whilst this process was taking place she fed them hot chocolate and biscuits. When asked what they were doing in the barn they answered that they had been walking with their parents and become lost. But the lady told her husband that the address on their shirt collars was Mile Oak LCC School, Portslade. He telephoned the police.

His wife gave them more chocolate and biscuits and as their fears subsided a knock was heard. It was Mr Brown from the school and he forced them into the back of a van and drove them back to the school. Fred was shown into the headmaster's study, made to bend over to touch his toes, then given six lashes of a cane. They were so painful they brought tears into his eyes. He was then ordered to follow the headmaster into the dormitory. To reach it they went through a long corridor, with toilets on either side, into a large room which must have held at least twenty beds. He was ordered to undress, put on a pair of pyjamas, and then led to a bed in the middle of the room. He did not sleep a wink that night. It was fear.

In the morning, as dawn was breaking, the light in the dormitory came on and a little Scotsman with white silvery hair came in shouting 'Wakey! Wakey! Rise and Shine! All is fine! Tuesday morning. Out of your beds.'

He stood and watched as the boys washed, dressed and made their beds. They were led into a large dining hall where each boy was given a place to sit. Grace was said. The head then announced that the school had been privileged to accept four new boys during the night. He read out the names and as the name of each boy was read out the boy had to stand up to be seen by the other boys. A meal was then served. Fred cannot remember the contents, but after the meal they were led into another room where hymns were sung and the headmaster preached a sermon. After the sermon they were led into a room for lessons.

A few weeks passed and he pleased the warders so much by his application to the teaching that they gave him permission to start a pigeon loft in the grounds. After he had been in the institution for nine months he was allowed out at times so he and his friend spent their time visiting the bonded warehouses in Portslade, hunting pigeons.

Unfortunately, there was one housemaster who interfered with the boys and when Fred was accosted by this man who tried to kiss him and interfere with him he went to the headmaster for help. The headmaster told Fred not to be stupid. He must have known this went on - Fred was never troubled again.

Fred and his friend, when they had escaped from the school on the first day, must have made a good impression on the farmer and his wife. The farmer had phoned the school several times since the incident enquiring about their welfare so the headmaster thought it a good idea for the boys now to be allowed to visit the farm on Saturday afternoons. The boys loved it. The farmer's wife entertained them with cakes and tea. The farmer taught them a good deal about farming. They were allowed to drive tractors, were taken to a farmers' show, and on one occasion were allowed to help in the delivery of a calf.

The problem was that Fred had not lost his mischievous streak. He and his friend decided to go to Portslade one night to rob a pigeon loft. They escaped from the school through the fire escape, and left it ajar with a piece of paper. Unfortunately the loft was alarmed and his friend was quickly caught but Fred managed to escape. He made his way back to school, climbed up the fire escape and was helped back by the headmaster who pulled him through - by his ear.

At morning assembly the two boys were made to pull down their trousers and were caned in front of the whole school. All privileges were stopped. Fred was made to serve the three years of the sentence. It was only towards the end of the time that he was allowed seven days' home leave. He was exactly thirteen years of age when he was released from the Approved School.

He found it difficult to settle down at home after his detention and continued his unruly behaviour. He was sentenced to three months' detention for driving a car without a licence and insurance, but managed to stay out of serious trouble until he was fifteen years old when he started work.

His first job was making copper electric switches for an engineering firm, in the Old Kent Road. Although he found a way of 'tea leafing' the copper from the factory he found the work boring so he left. He then went to work for 'Albert Harris', a tailor in Rye Lane, as a shop assistant. His friend's father had a shop that backed on to the tailor's, it was not long before ties, trousers, pants and jumpers were disappearing from the tailor's shelves and passed into his friend's establishment. Fred himself would often go home wearing three pairs of trousers. Mr Harris took stock one day and decided that Fred was not suitable to be employed as an assistant!

His next work was that of a packer in 'Louise Flowers' in Rye Lane. This firm produced nightdresses and dressing gowns; one Sunday afternoon he took a friend with him, put up a ladder at the back of the building and cleared the stock room. From this theft however he did not profit. The police were keeping a watch on him and, although the goods were in his friend's house, Fred thought it wise to keep his distance from the place.

His next job was with Pyes Transport, in Southampton Way, as an apprentice fitter. In this establishment he learned a good deal about lorries and alarm systems. He had friends in Parkstone Road, one who was on the run from the military police, so with them he now indulged in buying and selling stolen property. He was caught, sentenced to two years in a Borstal institution, in Latchmere House, Ham. Here he learned to be a motor mechanic and a better criminal. On being released from this institution he returned to civilian life and normal ways for a short time until once again was caught and sentenced for receiving stolen property.

He was sent to Reading Jail for six months. Everything here was done on the double! The orders were: no smoking, no talking, and physical training at 6.30 every morning before work. Four nights a week were spent on circuit training. They were housed in single cells, which had to be kept spotless. When an officer approached they had to stand to attention and shout out their name and number. The punishment for a misdemeanour, even smoking, was being locked up in the cell with just bread and water. Inmates were so distressed at the severe conditions that many slashed their wrists or swallowed needles. Fred thought that he would die in this prison! He came out determined never to go back.

In spite of his criminal record he managed to get a job in Gulf Garage, near the King's Arms, at Peckham Rye, repairing and servicing cars. As a matter of interest, as I write this story in 2005, the King's Arms, the large public house at the corner of Peckham Rye and East Dulwich Road, is now a block of flats. The owner of the Gulf Garage thought that Fred had a driving licence but Fred did nothing to make him aware that he did not. He took the test after six months, passed with no problems, driving the owner's Jaguar XJ6!

For the first time in his life Fred now felt a member of society. He felt legal! He met his first wife Margaret who already had a son, and settled down. He rented a house in Ashbourne Grove, East Dulwich, which was in a dilapidated condition and the owner put the house in the hands of the local estate agents. The agents regularly increased the rent to such an extent that Fred, in desperation, offered to buy it. He had done so much work on it that he thought he now had a right to own it. The agents refused his offers. Fred then destroyed the work he had done and called in the Council's health and safety department who ordered the agents to repair the damage. To make sure the agents received the correct message Fred removed slates from the roof and damaged the internal walls by spraying them for several hours with a hosepipe. Faced by the inspector of the Council who ordered repairs to the house, and a massive bill, the landlord agreed to sell the house to Fred.

Fred let the upstairs as a flat, to pay for the mortgage, and continued to work as a mechanic. As a known offender, he was well known to the local constabulary, who kept an eye on him. This close proximity and Fred's personality changed the attitude of the police who had contact with him. They now became his friends. One of them became so friendly that he would bring round confiscated pornographic videos which Fred would sell.

He was now in the 'big time' with the criminal fraternity and became friendly with the Richardsons - the well-known Camberwell criminals. He was buying and selling some of their 'products', also doing some work for them such as melting gold objects in one of their scrap metal yards, in the Old Kent Road.

His description of one of his jobs for the Richardsons is interesting. He would go to Birmingham and bring a lorry back containing anything from washing-up liquid to cigarettes. The goods had been bought by a loan firm and sold for less than half its value. He would deliver the load to a Richardson yard; the Richardsons had words for their activity, legal stealing. On one of these runs Fred was introduced to the Kray brothers in one of the Richardsons' yards. They asked him to do some work for them but he refused. He cannot explain why. For some unknown reason he took an immediate dislike to them. Many times on his journeys he felt that the police were on his trail but always managed to avoid being caught.

One day one of his friends told him that a lorry load of men's clothing had arrived at 7 Darrell Road, East Dulwich, and could be bought cheaply. He went there in his car as soon as he received the message but there was no one in. He went back at seven o'clock on the next evening. He remembers quite distinctly that the weather was terrible. It was very cold and the pouring rain soaked his clothes. He was apprehensive. Something about the place was not right. The house was dark. He parked his car opposite the house and waited, watching for movement. There was none. He went across the road and knocked again. The door was thrown open and four big muscular men came out and grabbed hold of him. He was taken into the kitchen and searched. His car keys were taken from him and he was handcuffed. It was only then that he was told he was in the hands of the police. He was ordered to sit down and keep perfectly quiet. Needless to say, he did as he was told.

Every now and again he could hear the front door bell ring. The door would be thrown open and the performance to which he had been subject- ed was repeated. The handcuffed men were made to join him in the kitchen. After some time the men were marched into the front two rooms of the house. He now saw that the rooms were stacked - from floor to ceiling - with men's clothes. One of the police officers gave him his car keys back. They were then marched to the front of the house where a Black Maria was waiting.   As they were preparing to leave one of the officers asked the others' whether the 'Roberts' car had been searched. On being told no, the officer asked for the car keys back. He took them, disappeared, then came back and gave Fred back his keys. The officer ordered Fred out of the van and led him back to his car. He opened the door, put his hand around the back of the driver's seat and pulled out four pairs of men's trousers - all brand new.

Fred was charged and went for trial at the Inner London Quarter Sessions. His lawyer found two witnesses who had, out of curiosity, watched the proceedings from a neighbouring house. They said, on oath, that they had seen two men from the raided house go to his car in the night, put something in the back and go back into the house. There was no driver in the car so he had obviously been a prisoner at the time. They then saw the handcuffed men being marched to the Black Maria. Fred pleaded that the police had planted the clothes and he thought the jury believed him because he was found not guilty. Fred was overjoyed. He was wrong to be happy. His joy was short lived! He was found not guilty of stealing the clothes in his car but guilty of receiving all the clothes in the house! He could not believe his ears! He was being found guilty for something he had not done. He was sentenced by the judge to two years in prison. He was taken down and locked up in one of the cells and later transferred to prison - Wormwood Scrubs.

His world disappeared. The prison was the worst he had been in, three grown-up men to a cell. Each one had his own piss pot . It was four weeks before he was able to have any contact with any member of his family or solicitor. From Wormwood Scrubs he was transferred to Bristol gaol and later to Rochester gaol on building courses. In the meantime, through his solicitor, he appealed against the conviction and sentence. His case was heard after a period of nine months at the Royal Courts of Justice in the Strand before three High Court Judges. They quashed the conviction as the case against him was unsafe and awarded him costs against the police. This was the princely sum of £150.00. If he wanted compensation for his internment he was told that he would have to bring an action against the police. He just wanted to be out of gaol. He believes that the police officers who had been involved in planting the stolen goods were dismissed from the force.

Fred went back to work as a self-employed builder and roofer - and was free from problems for two years.

Then his doorbell rang at six o'clock one morning. Two large policemen stood at the door.

'Are you Mr Wilfred Roberts?' they asked. 'Is that your Ford Consul estate car outside?'

'Yes.'

'Will you please come along with us .'

'What for?'

'Just come along with us.'

He dressed and accompanied the policemen to the police station where he was placed in a cell for an hour. Two policemen came in - one good cop and one bad cop.

The bad cop asked: 'Where did you steal the motor from Fred? What have you been up to Fred? You're really in it now. Probably get three years.'

'What are you talking about?' he said. 'I bought that car legally, with consent from your Sweeny car squad, three months ago. I have been coming into this *nick*, in that car, saying "hello" to the officers I know, for the past three months. No one has said a word about the car except P.C Robinson who remarked, "nice car you have Fred."   What the f...... hell is going on?'

The bad cop said: 'Don't tell us all that *bullshit*. We know you nicked the car.'

'Phone your Sweeny car squad, they will tell you,' replied Fred.

'You will be *banged up* quite a while for this. You will now be taken to Hendon police station to be interviewed,' said the bad cop.

The good cop had just listened and not said a word. Fred was handcuffed, taken to Hendon police station and put in a cell for three hours. Through the cell door he kept shouting his innocence; no one took any notice. The superintendent of the station then came down and took him into the interview room.

Fred explained how he had acquired the car.

'It was advertised in the Evening Standard car section for £1,500, which was cheap. Anyone interested should phone this number between 7 and 9 p.m. I phoned the number and a Mr Boulton answered. I arranged for him to bring the car to my second-hand shop in Barry Road the next evening at 8.30. The next day I realised that I could not keep the appointment so I phoned the number to alter the appointment. I had to ring several times that day before it was answered. When it was finally answered an old lady told me that I was phoning a telephone box in Edgware Road. I thought at the time, this is very dodgy. I went to East Dulwich Police Station. They too thought the matter strange. Nevertheless, they persuaded me to keep the appointment as previously arranged. They arranged for the Sweeney car squad to be with me when Mr Boulton came with the car.

'He arrived two hours late, as we were preparing to give up. As soon as he got out of the car the "Sweeney boys" swarmed all over him, and the car. They checked the car, the man, the log book and the engine number. Their finding was, "everything is fine, it's a good car, buy it Fred." I felt terrible having subjected this man to such an ordeal even though he appeared to be unperturbed by the event. In attempting to make amends for my inhospitality I invited him to my home for a drink. I still felt uneasy at the calm he displayed over the suffering he had endured. I felt it would be better if I did not buy the car. I said to him, "I now find that I can't raise £1,500. I can raise £1100 in cash tomorrow if you are interested." I thought he would get up and go. He did not. We arranged to meet at the Oval tube station the next day when I would hand him the money and he would give me the car and the log book. This is exactly what happened. He came the following day, gave me the car and log book and I handed over the money. End of story'.

The superintendent listened to the story without interruption. He took Fred back to the cell, where he was left for another hour. The superintendent returned full of apologies. He had checked out Fred's story and it was the truth. He was being released. When he asked to be given a lift back home it was refused. The reason given was that the superintendent was not authorised to do so. He had to take a cab home. He was furious. Not only had he been wrongfully arrested and spent a good deal of his time in police cells, it had cost him good money in the bargain. The car too had been impounded. He felt so strongly over the matter that he wrote to Esther Rantzen who put it on a show called "Watchdog". It was about how an international car thief had *hoodwinked* the police.

Fred's story of the purchase of the car is confirmed by a letter received to his solicitors from the Commissioners of Police of the Metropolis, New Scotland Yard in 1978. The letter states," the investigation has revealed no evidence that officers acted in other than the utmost good faith." Fred's claim that he was refused a lift home from Hendon Police Station is disputed by the sentence, "while it is appreciated that this conflicts with your clients version of what was said he trusts you will appreciate that in the absence of any disinterested witness he is unable to pursue this matter any further." The letter adds, "without admitting any liability, it would be appropriate in this case to make an ex-gratis payment of £162.00."

The company who owned the car, 'Rhinhewter UK Ltd.,' a German engineering company, on finding that the story had been televised, decided to let Fred have the car rather than face more publicity having to face him in court over ownership.

After this episode Fred's name was proposed for election to become a Freemason at a friend's lodge. With his convictions, he doubted whether his friend was sane even to suggest that his lodge would consider the application. He was astonished when he was accepted, even more so when he became master of the lodge - after only two years' membership.

One of the members was Mr Nash, who owned a jeweller's shop, in Bellenden Road. Interestingly, this man was well known to me as he and his family were patients of mine. His main occupation was that of a fence who bought and sold stolen goods. The police frequented his shop and I met them in his shop on many occasions when I was called to visit the shop to treat one of his family.

Mr Nash's shop was next door to Don's safe yard; Fred and his friends used the yard to get templates off, from different safes, which they were called upon to open.

Fred, now in poor health, was warned by the medical profession to contemplate his future so he decided to turn away from a world of crime and instability, blot out his past and retire to a life of normality. As he remarks, 'My young life was one of disgust, because my upbringing had taught me that this was normality.' It was being a freemason, mixing with people whose childhood had been different, which caused this transformation.

He started a building and burglar alarm company which Mr Jack Hause, an accountant, set up for him. He was taught by this man to play by the rules. This god- fearing man, who attended daily morning services at Streatham synagogue, was so much older than Fred that his influence on him was amazing. The age gap was so great can be gathered from the fact that Mr Hause, of blessed memory, died about three years ago at the ripe old age of 94. Fred is prepared to admit that he owes a lot to the fellow who educated him in good behaviour and that life has a meaning.

Although Wilfred, who became known as Fred, is in poor health he tries to help old people with small jobs, and from a life of being bent now goes straight. He often reflects about his past by the remark, 'I thought it was normal to behave in that fashion. Everyone I knew behaved like that.'

How Funny !

It was not possible to be in General Practice for forty-five years in a cosmopolitan area such as Peckham in South-East London without a sense of humour and I must be honest and say the patients often played tricks on me.

Hospitals in the 'fifties had a chain of command with a matron, deputy matron, staff nurses and nurses (slaves). The slaves walked in awe when approached by their superiors, shuddered when they passed and trembled at their commands. The matron was such a commanding figure that even the consultants treated her with the respect one gives to a dictator.

On visiting the Oldfield family in Lyndhurst Way in 1961, I was astonished by being asked by a shrieking lady, under the dining room table, to discuss the treatment I was giving her brother-in-law. Mr Oldfield had suffered a heart attack, was being cared for in a bedroom upstairs, and I had just come down the stairs on my way out of the house. At that time heart attacks were treated at home, with several weeks bed rest, followed by several weeks of convalescence.

The shrieking lady was seeking refuge from the three-year-old Oldfield boy who was attacking her with his little punches and she was attempting to evade his attacks. Needless to say I was very flippant with my answers, even though she told me that she was the deputy matron of Dulwich Hospital.

I had a hernia operation in Dulwich Hospital in 1963 and I noticed that my side ward was being specially spring-cleaned, the goddess of the hospital was coming to see me. It was customary for the matron to visit a GP. When she and her retinue duly appeared we passed the time quite pleasantly. On the following day, when the spring-cleaning was repeated, I was a little apprehensive. Perhaps the operation had not been a success. To my delight, the lady under the table in the Oldfield house appeared, dressed in her deputy-matron's uniform, with her retinue.

'You see,' she said; 'I really am the deputy matron of the hospital. The boy chasing me is my nephew; I am Mrs Oldfield's sister.'

Thank heavens Mr Oldfield recovered. It would have done my reputation no good at all had he succumbed.

My operation in itself was nothing to write about except I remember being given the 'premed' in the anaesthetic room and becoming very sleepy. I was wheeled from the anaesthetic room into the operating theatre, and while on the operating table I remember being asked by Mr Herriot , the surgeon, on which side the hernia was.

He was playing games with me for he was my old teacher at King's College Hospital. Although he was a most charming man he always wore the same serious expression. On waking up after the operation I examined both my groins very carefully to make sure he had operated on the correct side. He had!

On my visits to patients, dogs have sometimes been friendly, but they quickly realised I was not there to play nor did I fear them. After the initial bark they tended to ignore me.

On a home visit to Mr Blackmore in Brayards Road in 1962 my lack of fear of dogs paid off. The Blackmores had been patients of mine from my first day in Peckham but in nine years if they had required attention they had come to the surgery. They owned a sweetshop, and I had never crossed from the shop to the living accommodation before this request for a visit was made. I had visited the shop as a customer on many occasions to buy sweets for my children as it remained open until late at night. When Mr Blackmore did not serve in the shop his wife, or son, was in attendance. On this February evening the shop was still open at nine at night.

It was dark, cold and miserable outside; the shop was dimly lit. I went into the shop, the bell over the door clanged, the Blackmores therefore knew that they had a customer. No one however appeared behind the counter. I waited and waited. I opened the flap on the counter and slipped behind it. I opened the frosted-glass door separating the shop from the living accommodation to be met by a huge *Alsatian*, snarling and baring its teeth. In spite of its ferocious appearance, and the snarling, it slowly backed away. I pretended not to show any concern. As I took one apprehensive step forward, the animal took one step backwards. It growled, snarled and barked the whole time. It never took its eyes off me. Needless to say, apart from the barking and snarling, I was behaving in the same fashion. I never took my eyes off the beast for one second. I held my medical bag in front of me in case the animal should suddenly change its conduct and make a dash forwards, instead of backwards.

Mr Blackmore was lying on a couch at the end of the room and the dog, still snarling and baring its teeth, finally settled underneath him. To say that at this moment I was apprehensive at approaching the sick man's bed would be an understatement.

Mr Blackmore, quite ill, had apparently been dozing while the dog and I had played out our scene, but with the snarling immediately underneath him woke up and saw me.

He apologised for not being able to open the door. His wife had gone to a neighbour and I had arrived sooner than she expected.

He was in a pool of sweat. I too was in a pool of sweat. I wondered what part of my anatomy his dog would attack first when I came to examine its master. He had given no orders to the dog. I had to pretend to be brave and that nothing was amiss. I examined him while the dog continued a low-pitched growl under the couch.

'Normally he would have bitten you,' Mr Blackmore said, as I had my stethoscope on his chest listening to his heart - my eyes firmly fixed on the dog under the couch. I was shocked.

'Why didn't you tell me you had a dangerous animal?' I asked.

'No problem,' he answered. 'He would have been dangerous only if you had come last week. Today he is scared of you. You remind him too much of the vet who came a few days ago. He has a bag like yours and when the dog saw the bag he thought you were the vet. It appears to have the same smell.'

'We called the vet because the dog had an abscess in his mouth. When the vet called the dog attempted to attack him. The vet however is apparently used to this behaviour. He is a big muscular man. When the dog opened its mouth the vet grabbed the dog's head under his arm, saw the cause of the abscess was a bad tooth and yanked it out! The dog has backed away from you, he doesn't want to lose another tooth!'

Hannah Chesney Experienced Family Break Up

In 1989 Hannah Chesney told me the story of her bizarre upbringing. In spite of it she had still managed to reach the mature age of ninety-six years! I am sure the story of her life was related only as some sort of atonement for her rudeness to me in 1986, after my mother's death.

In 1986 I had followed the strict orthodox Jewish custom of not shaving for the first month after my mother's funeral. I had appeared at her home with a twenty-five days' growth of hair on my face. I had not expected to visit Hannah. I had been hoping that a visit to her would have been when I was clean-shaven and presentable. I was wrong!

She answered the door to me and stood shocked. She stared at my stubbly face in disbelief. She did not greet me with her usual smile, just pointed to my face and blurted out, 'What the hell do you think you're playing at? That can bloody well come off!'

After I had explained the reason for my unkempt facial appearance she was full of remorse. She did her best to comfort me at my loss. She apologised for her lack of knowledge of Jewish customs. When I told her that I intended to write a book of patients' lives she promised to give me her life story one day.

She kept her promise. Apart from the natural wear and tear which one expects with age, her memory of times and events was faultless. She even enjoyed having political discussions with me. She had arthritis but was still able to do her own housework! The only external help she needed was with her shopping and the local authority provided this. As she had all her faculties I enjoyed visiting her even though at times she was blunt to the point of rudeness.

Hannah was born in 1894 in Westmoreland Road, Walworth. Her father was known in the area as 'Handsome Jack', the lady-killer. When she was six years old he moved the family to Grosvener Terrace, Camberwell, and from that time she lost count of the number of times the family changed its address. She literally became a child of the streets, with a true Dickensian upbringing.

She never had a proper home. The furniture consisted of orange boxes and the family slept on old mattresses on the floor. Crockery did not exist. They used empty condensed milk bottles as cups. They would buy a tin of condensed milk for one halfpenny, take the lid off, and when empty, file down the edges to prevent cut lips. She knew that her father rarely paid rent, so the family would more often than not find itself homeless, thrown out into the street.

She was not an only child. She had an older brother and younger sister but there was no friendly relationship between the children. This was probably due to the fact that there was no relationship between the parents. Her father was a violent man who physically abused her mother. He would come home drunk, or after a night out with a girl friend, and demand food. When there was none available he would ask his wife for money to buy some. When both requests were met with refusals he would give her mother a beating. She knew that he often stole from her mother the means to entertain his lady friends. Hannah's hatred of her father began at an age when most girls have affection for Dad.

He came home one day and, being refused money, beat her mother so violently that she sustained a fractured jaw and was hospitalised. Her father now decided that with her mother in hospital he had no use for Hannah so he left home taking her brother and younger sister with him. She never saw her father again. Neither did she see her sister again until Hannah was married.

Hannah was now left on her own after her mother's hospitalisation, having to care for herself. She slept in the street at the entrance of their home in Westmoreland Road. Her grandmother came to visit on the following day, and not knowing of the family break up, took Hannah to live with her. She remained with her grandmother until she was twenty-one years old when she went into service as a housekeeper to an army officer's family.

Some years later she learned that her father, in a fit of temper, had killed her brother with a poker and been sentenced to a long term of imprisonment. She could not remember what the exact sentence was, also did not know what happened to him after he had served his sentence. I was rather distressed to hear that she hoped his end had been a bad one.

I found it rather sad that an old lady of such great age should feel so bitter and bear such hatred towards one of her parents. In normal circumstances, time or death, is usually the healer of such deep wounds.

———————

Accident Prevented Big Win

Harold Baker lived in Talfourd Road with his wife and family when I first had the good fortune to meet him in 1954. He came to register his family on my medical list with a smile on his face - and I can never remember that smile leaving his face until the day he died.

He and his wife lived in the same house for thirty years but after his wife died he found the house too large for him. His children had by this time married and left the area. Not only did he find the number of rooms too many for his purposes but he was lonely. To keep him company, he grew a long beard. I used to joke with him that it was not the beard but its occupants which provided him with the company he needed. He had always been a non-stop talker, now he had an audience!

I contacted the social services over his problems and we managed, after a good deal of effort, to arrange for him to be transferred to the sheltered accommodation unit on the North Peckham Estate. After all, he was seventy-eight years old when he was moved; he could not be accused of jumping any queues. His beard may have become longer and whiter but his pleasant smiling face and his cheerful outgoing behaviour could always be seen under the undergrowth. Having known him for such a long time had made our relationship a very close one. We were more than doctor and patient; we were the best of friends.

When he was eighty-one years old, and had been in sheltered accommodation for three years, his adventure on a pedestrian crossing on Peckham Road took place. Every year, since his retirement from work when sixty-five years old, he had spent the winter months with friends in Southern Ireland. Now he felt too old to go there in the winter. He was postponing his visit until June. He always went by boat. He explained to me that the crossing in the winter was too rough and exhausting for a man of his age. The sea was much smoother in June. There was no other reason. His friends still wanted him. There was an ongoing joke between us about his relationship with the Southern Irish that when he returned, trouble always broke out in Northern Ireland. I complained that the reason he went to Eire was to stir things up! It was therefore only his age that explained why Harold was still in Peckham in January 1988 and not on a farm in Tipperary.

Harold was a betting man. He loved horses and the pleasure of horse racing. As I have already mentioned, I had never seen Harold without a smile on his face. Even when his daily bets had failed to provide him with a single winner, he still had a beam on his face. The betting shop is a very welcoming place for an old man who is fond of a small wager, knows when to curb his passion when on a winning run, and does not put his pension on a certain winner - that comes last!

It was therefore not odd to find Harold crossing the Peckham Road on his way to the betting shop from his home in the sheltered accommodation on the North Peckham Estate one mild January morning in 1988. He was making his way on a zebra crossing when the accident occurred. It could not be said that he was anyway to blame. He was at the rear of a long line of children on their way from Oliver Goldsmith School. A policeman on duty at this crossing was monitoring their passage across the road!

A car that had failed to pull up in time knocked Harold down - at the rear of the procession - with a newspaper in his hand and his forecasts in his pocket. He had not noticed the car. To be honest, when he related the story to me he admitted that the last thing on his mind had been cars. A policeman was actually giving him permission to cross!

He lay on the ground screaming in agony! He had sustained, as we learned later from the hospital reports, a fractured femur. His absence of a detailed knowledge of anatomy did not worry him at the time. All he knew was that he was suffering agonising pain in his right hip joint. Not only was the pain intense, it was magnified by the knowledge that he had been attacked on a police-monitored crossing. He had felt so safe! He had done the same journey, with the same children, at the same crossing, at the same time, dozens of times, in perfect safety.

The policeman was beside himself with fury at the driver of the car. It was a lady. When Harold first looked up she was standing in the road crying, hysterical, shaking with fright. She was sobbing so loudly that the policeman was having difficulty in getting information from her. Even though Harold was in such severe pain and not particularly interested in the conversation he could see that the policeman was becoming more frustrated and rapidly losing patience. The crowd of inquisitive children who were giving advice as to how the accident had occurred, and how he should conduct his enquiries were also not helping him. Harold too had his problems with the children; he had to fend them off as they persistently tried to get him up.

A large crowd had now gathered. The main road was blocked. Long distance lorry drivers from the continent, who used this road from Dover to Central London not knowing of the accident, must have been cursing whoever was causing this delay.

As Harold told me the story from his hospital bed he said, 'it was a real pantomime'. He would have enjoyed it, had he not been in so much pain.

The policeman was taking turns in shouting questions at him as he lay on the ground, then at the driver of the car. Both were in a state of shock, in no fit state to provide him with answers. The crowd gathered around looked on as if it was a play and ready to clap the performance at any moment. The policeman too was evidently in shock. Having made up his mind that Harold was old, he assumed that he was deaf too. Harold's hearing suffered for days as a result of this assumption. The questioning consisted of the policeman standing up to question the lady driver then stooping down to bellow in poor Harold's ear.

When he related the story his precise words were, 'you know doc., that copper was making a hell of a racket!'

The cause of all the commotion, the driver of the car, had by this time been reduced to the state of a blithering idiot. A chair from Kennedy's, the cooked meat shop, had to be brought out for her to sit down.

The impasse was resolved only when an ambulance arrived. The two ambulance men tried to pacify Harold, with little result. He screamed in agony as they tried to move him while the policeman, completely oblivious to his shrieking, continued to bellow questions in his ear. Although in agonising pain, he was finally coaxed on to a stretcher. With klaxon sounding he was transported to the casualty department of King's College Hospital.

A few days after the accident, when Harold had somewhat recovered from the shock and his leg had been pinned, he checked the racing results of the day of the accident. The true significance of the events of that tragic day hit him.

He had asked the sister of the ward whether it would be possible for her to get a copy of a newspaper of the day after his admission. It had to be for that day; no other paper would suffice. He would be satisfied with any newspaper. She said that she would try, but doubted whether his accident would be reported. His accident was a commonplace one. He did not tell her the real reason. He feared that if she knew she might not be prepared to make the effort. That evening she triumphantly returned with a copy of The Daily Mirror.

On the day of the accident he had been on his way to the betting shop, not returning from it! His forecasts were still in his jacket pocket. He had been unable to place his bets. As he lay in his bed nursing his broken leg and looked at the racing results printed in the newspaper of that day he broke out in a sweat. He had done a *five horse Yankee*, three of the horses running at odds of 9-1 and two horses at 8-1. Every one of the horses had won! Had he reached the betting shop his winnings would have amounted to £43,000, for his 50p bet! The lady driver had robbed him of a fortune!

It was not to be. Fortune was determined not to smile on him. I explained that what had happened made one believe in God. Should he have won such large amount of money, at his advanced age, he would have become a good-for-nothing layabout. He might have squandered his money on drink or become a capitalist of the worst possible kind. He might even have died of shock!

The lady who had knocked him down had obviously been sent to do the deed by the Almighty. She was probably the bookie's wife and saved her husband from disaster too. He would never have believed he could have lost so much money for just a 50p bet. The odds against Harold winning had been so great he would not have bothered to lay the bet off. He would have been prepared to cover it himself. On finding that Harold had won so much money for such an insignificant amount he would almost certainly have shot himself. Not only had Harold himself been saved another man's life had been saved too.

Harold remained unperturbed during my explanation. He remained with the same smile on his face which had enchanted me for the thirty-four years of our acquaintance. He put his hand into his breast pocket and took out a crumpled sheet of a paper, the betting slip, which he proudly showed to me. He then gave me the page of the newspaper that gave the racing results of that day. This was proof that if he had made it to the bookmaker he would have become a rich man.

The money would indeed not have helped Harold very much. Eighteen months after the accident he suffered a stroke, which proved fatal.

May his dear soul rest in peace.

What A Life In Peckham !

Holly Grove crosses Bellenden Road and its shrubbery over a hundred years old leads to Rye Lane which is the main shopping centre in Peckham. Holly Grove has several houses of character that time has not changed.

Facing the shrubbery, the house with the wooden entrance door to the basement covered on its backside with iron plate intrigued me the most. It was number twenty-two and at the time of this story it was owned by Mrs John. I was told that the iron- clad door had been made in this fashion when the house was built to prevent highwaymen who might have tried to hack the door down from the outside. The house had been built in 1840 but, I must be honest, I did not know that highwaymen still haunted Peckham as late as this. Mr John had bought the house in 1913, but I never knew this gentleman, he had departed this life long before my arrival in Peckham.

Mrs John was a shrivelled up, miserly old lady in her eighties, who bought only six pennyworths of chips from the local fish and chip shop, even though everyone knew her to be a very wealthy woman. It was common knowledge that Mr John had left his *missus* well provided for! The six pennyworth of chips bought for her on Monday by her tenant Mrs Runacre was made to last the whole week. To save money on the gas bill she boiled six eggs on Monday. In this way she organised for herself six suppers for the week. Her diet never varied. One pennyworth of chips and one egg for supper every weekday. Sunday was the Lord's Day; she splashed out a little, and allowed herself a lamb chop.

When in 1954 she took ill and I prescribed a greater variety to her diet she told me that this was impossible; she was saving her money. The greatest thrill in her life would be after she was dead if she were able to leave a larger inheritance to her grandson than his other grandparents. Her logic defeated me; how would she know after she was dead?

She rented the basement of her house to the Runacres and there was no love lost between the landlady and her tenants. Mrs John spent all her waking hours in working out ways of saving money and made it her duty that the Runacres knew they were not to be allowed to waste any of it! They considered her parsimonious behaviour was due to her age and would run errands for the old lady as acts of kindness. Indeed, they were the culprits who went every Monday to the fish and chip shop to purchase her weekly supply. Mrs John was in her eighties. Theirs were acts of benevolence and they had not seen her will! I had been a witness to it; there was only one beneficiary - her grandson.

The Runacres had moved into the basement of 22 Holly Grove in 1945. As Mr Runacre departed this life in 1956, his wife - who was in her fifties - had to cope with an impossible situation. She was in the unenviable position of not being able to afford to move, having accommodation most unsuitable for her growing family, and a landlady who was not prepared to let her rent one of her empty rooms on the ground floor. This was one occasion when Mrs John's malevolence was greater than her stinginess.

Mrs Runacre and family were forced to live in damp, cramp conditions until 1960 when the good Lord took Mrs John into his keeping and the family - without permission - moved from the damp basement, upstairs. There then proceeded a long and bitter court case over possession of the property in which I became involved as Mrs Runacre's doctor. Mrs Runacre won in the end, as she had been a tenant since 1945 but the court's findings only gave her the right to remain upstairs while she herself remained in the building. Her family were given no rights. As Mrs Runacre was old it could be said that both parties were victorious.

Mrs Runacre lived until 1981 so had many years living in a dry environment. When she died Mrs John's dreams were fulfilled; her heir took over the whole of the house. She can indeed rest in peace - she had managed to leave her grandson more than his other grandparents did.

The shrubbery that was facing number 22 Holly Grove was, as its name implies, a small park filled with shrubs. When the Johns' had bought the house this was a private park owned by the tenants of The Grove and kept locked. Each householder in the Grove had a key; the common herd were kept out! The Shrubbery has long since changed its character. It is now a public park, a home for birds and a meeting and sleeping place for many desirable and undesirable characters. The memory of the past still lingers as the gates and railings that were removed in the 1939-45 war have long since been replaced, and the gates were locked at night for a time.

Next door to the Runacres lived Mr and Mrs Moorgate who joined my medical list in 1962. They were a couple in their late forties who had worked for the colonial service and had just returned from a period of service in the backwoods of South America.

In June of that year I had an occasion to visit Mr Moorgate and it was an experience that I have never forgotten. I went upstairs to the bedroom and, knowing the previous residences of the Moorgates, I was not surprised to find various totem poles, drums, and other knickknacks on my way up the stairs. What shocked me was to find a wooden coffin underneath the window bay of his bedroom. Lying in bed he could dream of his future!

I looked at the patient, looked at his wife, looked at the coffin, and with a grin on my face said to Mrs Moorgate, 'it's pointless examining your old man, or giving you a prescription as you've got everything stitched up. If you hang on, I will go to the surgery and bring a death certificate back with me. It will save me another call!' I knew the couple well, knew that they had a sense of humour similar to mine, otherwise I would have been in serious trouble for making such facetious remarks.

Mr Moorgate now gave me the history of the coffin. It was not a fake; it was a real one made of sandalwood with solid wood handles. It was now being used by them as a chest for storing linen but had not been originally obtained for this purpose. It had been bought for Mr Moorgate when he contracted Sandfly fever whilst working in one of the remote villages in the mountains of South America. What a British civil servant should be doing in such a remote place I thought it wise not to ask. As he did not volunteer the information I listened thinking it prudent not to question.

He had been in the place two years when he was struck down. People in the area died so quickly of Sandfly fever it was customary for a coffin to be made for the sufferer as soon as he contracted the disease. The symptoms of this complaint are similar to that of Dengue Fever, which is more common, and caused by a mosquito bite. Most of the sufferers made use of their coffins, but Mr Moorgate, a tough bloody-minded Englishman did not, according to the locals, have the decency to fill it. He was one of the survivors. Rather than waste a good wooden container he had brought it home with him and used it as a chest for storing linen. It still had the baggage labels affixed to its sides because on the boat home it had been used as a cabin trunk.

The Moorgates had no intention of disposing of it. One day it was going to save them money by using it for its proper purpose! Thankfully I was saved the prospect of having to argue with them over its use as they moved in 1978 and I have since had no contact with them.

I don't believe I would have the courage to sleep in the same room as my ultimate resting place however much money I was going to save!

———

I was driving along Nunhead Lane at 11.30 one morning in April 1966 when I was caught in a police speed trap. I had turned left from Linden Grove into Nunhead Lane and as the present traffic lights at this junction had yet to be   installed I was speeding along nonchalantly towards Peckham Rye when a policeman suddenly appeared in the road blocking my path. There is a bend in the road at this point and the policeman appeared as out of thin air between two parked cars. I would have knocked him down had I not stopped. He had a notebook in his hand but his face turned pale when he recognised me. I could see the look of horror on his face.

'My God, it's the doctor!'

I did not recognise him and thought that he had identified me from the badge on my windscreen. I was soon made aware that this was not so. He had recognised me as the doctor who had attended his wife the previous night at the delivery of a little girl. I had been summoned by Sister Kenny, one of the local midwives, to attend to his wife as an emergency and had spent most of the night in his house in Consort Road. His wife was not a patient of mine and I had never seen the couple before but I was a doctor who practised maternity for home deliveries. This policeman had presumably had time to remember my features because of the length of time I had spent in his house.

He had been present at the birth. I had been so involved with his wife's delivery that I did not remember his face and we wore masks at the actual delivery. This man who stopped me was a policeman; uniform always appears to alter a person's appearance.

The policeman, PC Jarvis, explained to me that the sergeant on duty with him in the speed trap was not friendly to doctors in his present mood. He would do his best for me but would not make any promises.

'The sergeant is in a terrible mood. For God's sake keep quiet. Leave it all to me. Say nothing doc.'

I did not answer. He was acting the perfect policeman, authority with dignity. I had not recognised him, so did not understand why he would be so conciliatory in trying to protect me from the dreaded sergeant.

The sergeant, in plain clothes, was walking towards me, but had not yet reached the car when the constable hastened to leave me and intercept him.

The set up of the speed trap was that the sergeant stood at the first checkpoint with a stopwatch. A second policeman stood at a set distance with a stopwatch at a second checkpoint. My policeman (PC Jarvis) stood at a point further on. When a motorist was found to have exceeded the speed limit, PC Jarvis was signalled to stop the car. Although my policeman had recognised me he had done his duty and stopped me.

PC Jarvis and the sergeant came up to my car walking together and I could see that the sergeant had a disturbed, thunderous look on his face. Although the sergeant was in plain clothes, had he not been with PC Jarvis, I would still have known that he was in the police force. Only people in authority walk in this fashion. Every sergeant major I encountered in my army service walked this way. This sergeant walked with slow, even, deliberate, intimidating steps - each step exactly the same length to the inch as the previous one.

I remained in the driver's seat of my car with the window turned down as the pair conferred while standing in the road looking down at me. I could hear the conversation quite clearly. PC Jarvis was explaining to the sergeant that I was a doctor on an urgent visit. I was in a hurry as I had spent most of the previous night attending to his wife; this had caused me problems with my work schedule. Now I knew why he was trying to shield me!

He was so apologetic, his phraseology so servile, that even I squirmed. The sergeant listened pensively, his left hand stroking his face as he listened to the recital of my problems. When PC Jarvis had completed his obsequious speech the sergeant put his head through my car window, glared at me for what appeared to be an eternity, then proceeded to give me a lecture. In a restrained voice he ordered me to curb my speed in the future in built up areas.

'You're a doctor,' he said. 'I know you are not a bloody fool, otherwise the police constable would not have spoken so highly of you. Why, when you know the speed limit in built up areas is thirty miles an hour, don't you stick to it?'

I just sat in the driver's seat shamefaced, saying 'yes sergeant, no sergeant,' whenever I thought it judicious to say so. He ended the conversation by saying crossly, 'now don't write to thank me for not booking you!'

This last statement foxed me. I did not understand the implication of this remark but thought it prudent to sit silent. He waved me on. I did not hesitate to drive away at the fastest permissible speed.

I had forgotten all about the incident until I went to see PC Jarvis' wife that evening and the police constable was at home to open the door to me. He explained that I had been extremely lucky at not being booked for a speeding offence that day. Even he did not think he could have persuaded the sergeant to let me go just with a caution.

An Indian doctor had a similar incident to mine, driving over the speed limit, three weeks previously and the sergeant - always merciful to doctors - had sent him away with a caution. The doctor had then written a thank you letter to the superintendent of the police station praising the sergeant. In his letter he praised the sergeant who had been in plain clothes, the two policemen in uniform and the queen for being the head of such a wonderful nation. He praised the government who had such a fine body of men to protect the country and the quality and professionalism of the British police for only cautioning him for a speeding offence. The one person he had forgotten to praise in his letter was the superintendent. It would have made no difference!

The sergeant had received a dressing down from the superintendent reminding him that he was not the chief of the police. He was not even a superintendent! He was not a magistrate nor was he a judge. It was not for him to decide whether to take action or just caution a speeding motorist. His job was just to book a speeding motorist and leave his elders and betters to decide what action to take.

PC Jarvis and the other policeman in the trap had known of the dressing down the sergeant had received. When they realised another doctor had been trapped in the sergeant's net they had expected anything except a merciful outcome.

Time had perhaps healed the wound a little. Two weeks had elapsed since the dressing down and being PC Jarvis' doctor at his wife's confinement had softened his resolve to mete out the death penalty. I had evidently been a lucky doctor that day.

————————

By coincidence, I had another interesting experience in 1966 whilst driving along Nunhead Lane. It was six months after my brush with the police. This time it was while driving in the opposite direction - from

Peckham Rye towards Consort Road. I had just negotiated the bend in the road opposite Barforth Road, a few yards from where on the opposite side of the road I had been previously been caught in a speed trap. To my surprise, I saw an elderly man sitting halfway up a broken wall at the corner of Consort Road and Nunhead Lane. This brick wall had been complete when I had driven through on the previous day. It has long since disappeared with the redevelopment of the area but must have been seven feet high. The top half had been demolished and the old man was perched about four feet above the ground on the jagged, bottom section. A load of bricks scattered indiscriminately all over the pavement under the wall showed that an accident had just occurred.

I could not believe my eyes! There appeared to be no traffic in the area. No cars. No person in sight. No noise. There was just this little old man sitting on top of a half knocked-down wall. To describe him as sitting is not quite correct; he was more bent double than sitting. He was facing the road and kept moving his head from side to side as if he was trying to recognise something.

I stopped and got out of my car before I reached the spot. It was eerie. Everything appeared unreal. I thought it might be a film set but there were neither cameras nor lights to be seen. It was then I saw and heard a lorry backing into Linden Grove from Nunhead Lane. It had, as I later learned, hit this man, knocked down the top of the wall, and left him suspended on the unbroken section. The wall must have been in a pretty bad state for it to disintegrate on impact. This was fortunate for the little old man otherwise he would most certainly have been crushed to death.

I helped the old fellow from the wall and brushed him down as best I could for he was covered in dust from head to foot. He was shaken and shocked. All answers to my questions produced only one answer, 'I am all right, and can you please take me home'!

Who would not have wanted to go home after having had an argument with a ten ton lorry? From his appearance he looked as if he could do with a hospital check up. Although he did not tell me what had happened, he insisted that he was all right and wanted to go home. Though I tried hard to persuade him to go to hospital he adamantly refused. It was then I had to be stubborn myself. If I made it a condition that I took him home first to tell his wife that he was well and not to worry would he allow me to take him to the casualty department of Dulwich Hospital? He agreed, so I took him home. In spite of pleadings from both his wife and himself that it was unnecessary, I took him to the casualty department. I explained to the casualty officer what I had found and asked him to notify the police.

I drove back along Nunhead Lane to do the home visits which had brought me along this route in the first place. On reaching the spot where the accident had occurred I found a large crowd had gathered. Also in the immediate vicinity were two police cars, an ambulance with its doors opened wide, a recovery van, a fire engine and a lorry. All the occupants of these vehicles were looking for an injured man who had been spirited away by an unknown force.

The lorry driver who had knocked the man down had reported the accident to the police. He had given them his version of the accident. His brakes had failed as he had approached the junction of Linden Grove and Nunhead Lane. He believed that he had knocked a man down, but was now not too sure. He had searched and searched but could not find the fellow.

He had tried to avoid hitting a man who was crossing the road when his brakes had locked. By doing so, the lorry had skidded and crashed into the wall in Nunhead Lane. When his lorry had come to a stop he could swear that he had hit a fellow. There was someone sitting on the wall and the top of the wall had collapsed. He had backed his lorry into Linden Grove to rescue him. When he got down from his lorry the chap had disappeared. He thought that he must have fallen backwards on to the other side of the wall and had done the right thing by notifying the police. He had then gone to help the fellow but could not find him. The fellow could not have been seriously injured if he had got up and walked away. He was now beginning to wonder whether the accident had affected his mental state. I suppose he was hoping that it was all a bad dream and that he would soon wake up.

I stopped. I explained to the police that I was the unknown force who had spirited the victim away and where he could now be found. The police thanked me for my prompt assistance and, in the usual way, asked for my name and address. In hindsight, having done my bit of first aid, I should have avoided Nunhead Lane and taken another route to visit my patients.

The victim was not a patient of mine but out of interest I telephoned the hospital a few days later to find out what the casualty officer had done and what injuries the man had sustained. I learned that the fellow had been examined head to foot and been X-rayed, but having no broken bones had been discharged with a letter for his GP. The man had sustained only superficial bruising and denied that he had ever lost consciousness so the hospital had no alternative except to accede to the man's wishes and allow him to return home. As with all matters which were no longer my concern I forgot all about the incident. It went completely out of my mind. I was very busy in my practice so this was just one event in a busy daily work schedule.

In 1969, three years after the experience of the broken wall, a firm of solicitors wrote to me asking for a report on the injuries sustained by their client. He was now making a claim against the lorry driver. I had made only a superficial examination of the fellow at the scene of the accident, as any person doing first aid might do; my report was therefore a short one. The solicitors were not satisfied. They wrote to me again questioning my findings. They were obviously trying to get me to write that I had found the fellow half dead. I replied that I had nothing to add to my previous letter and received no further communication from them until nine months later when I was *subpoenaed* to appear in court as a witness.

Barristers are actors, can make or break a witness and have it in their power, if they are good and have expertise, to make one look so foolish as to make one want to run away and hide. I will never forget my appearance in that court. I had a horrible time. Over forty years have passed and I have given evidence many times. Even writing about this case, after all this time, evokes painful memories.

The barrister, representing the old fellow, resented my evidence that his client was conscious when I took him off the rubble of the broken-down wall. He was attempting to throw doubts on my memory of events that had taken place three years previously. At the time, it seemed to me, that I was being accused of giving false evidence.

'Surely doctor, you do not expect me to believe that this frail old man, you see him sitting here,' - he then pointed to the old man who appeared to have aged twenty years in the three years since I had last seen him - 'was fully in charge of his faculties after having suffered such a serious accident?'

He paused after every short statement. His speech was staccato, like sharp rapier thrusts. Now I was the victim. I was being made to look a fool or a liar. I winced after every one of his statements.

'The wall was knocked down, doctor! A solid, brick, seven foot wall, which had withstood the Blitz, doctor!'

Here he made a very lengthy pause. He looked at the judge. Then he looked at me.

'The lorry was a ten tonner! It had skidded, doctor! The man was in the middle of the road, doctor!'

He continued. 'This lorry was travelling at speed. The driver had seen the old man and tried to stop. He found his brakes had failed. He did all he could to avoid an accident, but the lorry skidded! He knocked the old man down. He knocked the man into the wall. The top of the wall fell down, doctor! He was suspended on top of the wall that remained! You still insist that he was conscious and able to speak to you, doctor?'

The barrister was using short sharp sentences, to give maximum effect to his oratory. It was obvious to me that he was doing his best to cast doubt on my evidence. I was being made to appear in the barrister's opinion to be lying, being paid by the defendants, or mentally defective for sticking to my evidence. I could only tell the truth. As I continued to stick to my own version of what I had seen and done the hostility shown to me by the barrister was almost more than I could bear.

The barrister was obviously doing his best to break me. He was succeeding. I was being ground into fine powder as in a mill. My mind was in a whirl. I was having problems in answering his questions. I reverted to the stammer from which I had suffered as a boy. I was not used to being in court, and when I had been, I had not been treated as a hostile witness. Whenever I had previously made a court appearance I had been treated with respect and friendliness. Now I was being attacked. The judge too was allowing my persecution to continue without interference.

The barrister was after all only doing his duty. He was not medically qualified. An old man perched on top of a broken-down wall, placed there by a ten-ton lorry, must have given him a field day for his acting abilities. I don't suppose for one moment he personally bore me any malice. In court, however, from the way he kept looking at me you would have thought that he even resented the air I breathed.

When I was allowed to leave the witness box and was told that my presence in the court would no longer be required, I fled. To this day, I do not know how the case ended or how much the old man received in compensation.

My mind was in turmoil as I left the witness box. I just wanted to forget that I had ever been involved. I had simply stopped to help a poor chap who had been knocked down and was stuck on a broken-down wall. This was the reward for my good deed!

I was so distressed that I did not even stop to collect the fee for my court appearance!

Man Wanted Sex Change

The practice in Bellenden Road, being in existence for forty-five years in a mixed working class area, had many strange patients; none perhaps as odd as Jaynee Lee. This was not his real name. His real Christian name was John, but he insisted on being called Jaynee. He was a patient of one of my partners and at the age of forty-six years came to see Dr Cook requesting a sex change. Dr Cook knew this man well as he had treated him for a number of years. He also knew that he was a transvestite. But the demand for a sex change was new. His answer to this request was concise.

'You must be crazy to want a sex change at your age, you will be right in the middle of your change!'

My partner was correct. John was indeed crazy. John, now repeatedly refused help from my partner, transferred his attention to me and proceeded to drive me mad to get a sex change. He wanted to be a woman and would not accept the fact that the National Health Service, at the time, would not provide the funds for this operation. He dressed like a woman, pretended to behave like one, and insisted that he required to take the contraceptive pill. It was no use my trying to persuade him that at the age of forty-six he (she) would not be likely to conceive. In any event he had no partner! To keep him quiet and prevent him reporting me with a complaint to the authorities I reluctantly prescribed contraceptives for him. My reason for this was that he said he was in the menopause and he had read in a magazine that the contraceptive pill was the only tablet which helped. I also prescribed tablets for his mental state!

I believed that the only way to placate this man and get him off my back was to refer him to a psychiatrist. I found to my cost that I wasted my time. The psychiatrist I referred him to was of little help. He prescribed anti-depressants for him, counselled him about his aberration, but sent him back to me for treatment.

John(Jaynee) used to waste my time with utter nonsense, he was the ultimate in looniness. He would insist on seeing me whenever he read in a newspaper that the pill had side effects or a patient blamed the pill for her illness. Newspapers sell by sensational reporting. If a girl on the pill develops a hump in Alaska it makes headlines, if she is taking the contraceptive pill it obviously has to be the cause. He would avidly read the

91

newspapers trying to find in them any new information about the pill or sex change. If he did, I was in for a restless and troublesome fortnight. I had the dubious task of persuading him on numerous occasions that he would come to no harm on the contraceptive pill that I was prescribing for him.

On one occasion he came to see me in a terrible state after reading in a newspaper a medical report linking cancer of the cervix (neck of womb) with the pill being prescribed for him. He complained of lassitude, pain in the lower part of his abdomen and dysuria - and demanded to know whether the pill that he was being prescribed could cause him to have cancer of the uterus. As he did not have a womb this stunned my perception of his problem and caused me to think for a moment. When I realised that he had not understood the medical terms used I could honestly reassure him that his 'female' parts were not in jeopardy.

John(Jaynee Lee) had a face which always looked as if it needed a shave, so to cover the stubble, he added a thick layer of powder. He wore lipstick, grew his hair long, but forgot that he had a moustache! High heels, long plastic boots, a mini-skirt displaying hairy legs, and a shoulder bag completed his ensemble. The Almighty appeared to side with me about John. He too obviously disapproved of his attempts to become a female; he gave him a deep bass voice. When this apparition called Jaynee Lee spoke, anyone who had not previously met him listened in stunned silence.

I will always remember the first time we met in 1978; I was returning from visiting a patient and having parked my car outside the surgery I walked to the front door. He was sitting on the front doorstep waiting for the door to be opened for the afternoon surgery. I clearly did not see the female part of this creature, only his head and moustache. In my normal nonsensical way I called out,

'Good afternoon, Sir!'

He jumped up as if he had been shot. I thought he was going to hit me. His violent reaction caused me to look again.

This time without batting an eyelid I said, 'Sorry, good afternoon, Madam!'

He grinned and sat down. He was satisfied that I had established his true gender.

The trouble with the man was that he was a chatterbox, a non-stop talker, who would sit in the waiting room chatting to the other patients while waiting to see me.

The patients would sit uncomfortably, making every effort to ignore him. I opened the consulting room door one evening to see a little black boy, who was usually a nuisance in the waiting room when he came to see me, sitting quietly, bolt upright, with his mouth wide open in wonderment. It was strange. Whenever this boy had previously attended I had quickly been made aware of his presence.

The boy, now quiet as a dormouse, was sitting on the right of the room and I just had to follow the boy's eyes to see what had caused his deafening silence. He was looking at this strange creature in a mini-skirt and hairy legs. The boy's eyes were on *organ stops!* He was holding his mother's hand tightly, wondering what this strange animal was. John was talking to the boy, but the boy was too terrified to answer.

Unfortunately, looking so strange and behaving so oddly made John become a victim of scavengers and layabouts who tormented him and made his life an absolute misery. He was to these tormentors an object of ridicule. They would write graffiti on the front door of his flat in Kirkwood Road so that passers-by would know what type of man the occupant was. There was a notice in white paint on the door which read: 'The crazy man or woman lives here - please knock hard!'

The final period of John's life was when drug abusers moved into his flat. John had one serious medical problem: he was an asthmatic. When I had to make a visit one day I found the flat had been turned into a squalid dump. It had nine teenage residents, black and white, all doped up to the eyeballs, lying about the place. He was apparently unable by normal means to rid himself of these new friends so in desperation turned to abnormal means. He burned the flat down.

One day, his neighbours smelt burning, and saw the passageway of the block filled with smoke so they phoned the fire brigade. When the fire brigade arrived, John (Janeey Lee) was found quietly sitting on the steps to the entrance of the block rolling a cigarette, humming to himself. He had finally flipped! The police were called and John was sent into a mental institution.

My partner in the practice was right! John should not have wished to change his sex in the middle of the change. Sadly, I learned a few years later that John had died in an asthma attack in a hospital.

Encounters With Witchcraft

Jimmy, a friendly black man from Sierra Leone, with a grin which extended from ear to ear and never left it, lived in Crofton Road, Camberwell, in 1977.

He had worked for the British in Africa as a railwayman. When the British gave his country independence he continued under the new regime then - when he retired in 1975 - came to live in this country.

He had one wife and she was a patient of mine until the couple divorced and she moved out of the area. He boasted of several concubines whom he had left behind in Africa. I use the word 'concubine' in the biblical sense. Jimmy called them wives, but the wife who had accompanied him to this country always refused to accept them in this category.

These wives (concubines) had produced children for Jimmy. To his credit he went back occasionally to see them and provide them with money which on his pension he could ill afford. Although I asked him on many occasions why he had come to this country after he retired - he always grumbled to me about our weather - he refused to tell me. My original guess was wives trouble, but after getting to know him better I wondered if it had something to do with witchcraft.

In 1979 he developed heart failure, which resulted in my having to make many visits to his home and I got to know him very well. We became friends. By the time he had his heart trouble he had already divorced his wife in this country. I cannot remember who instituted proceedings, but when the event I am about to relate occurred he lived alone, with only friends to attend to his needs.

He lived upstairs on the first floor of a house that had been converted into flats. In his dining room were placed obelisks (small stone pillars about eighteen inches high) on the floor. There were about a dozen of them. They looked like small gravestones, and they were placed around the room in some sort of a peculiar pattern. Not being familiar with African culture, and perhaps not willing to question his beliefs, I at first pretended not to notice these objects. On becoming friendlier, I began to question him as to the reason for the objects on the floor.

He now gave me a thirty-minute lecture on African culture, the part the witch doctor played, and the nature of his performance. I learned that tribal Africans hated and avoided hospitals. They regard where a person dies as a place of bad luck, and as many people unavoidably die in hospital, it is a place of ill omen - best avoided.

This perhaps explains why witchcraft still cannot be eradicated in parts of Africa.

I now learned the reason for the obelisks. They were something to do with his part-time occupation: he practised witchcraft. Many of his friends came to him to make use of his services. They came to him to cast spells on their enemies and he obliged them. I listened to him spellbound. It was the first time in my life I had met a real-life witch doctor, even though the witch doctor was masquerading in western clothes. I was fascinated and intrigued that although Jimmy practised his beliefs he still expected me to cure him. It was an eye opener to me that Jimmy, whom I had always been given to believe to be a practising Christian, could actually believe in such pagan creeds.

I now asked him as a special favour to me to cast a spell on my mother-in law. She was someone I could not bear the sight of. I would love to see her suffer the same torments which she daily handed out to my long-suffering father-in-law. If Jimmy were successful, I was certain that when my father-in-law knew whom his saviour was he would reward Jimmy well. My father-in-law was a rich man. He would be much richer if his wife did not spend all his money. Jimmy had been wise to tell me his profession. I was about to make Jimmy a rich witch doctor.

Jimmy listened to me without saying a word, then asked me my mother-in law's name.

'Sarah,' I said.

'How old is she?'

'About seventy. No, exactly sixty-nine years and six months.'

I had already got the message that witchcraft was a precise art and could not work on approximation!

'Dark or fair?' he continued.

'Dark.'

'Short or tall?'

'Short.'

'Round or oval face?'

'Round-faced.'

'Fine,' said Jimmy. 'I've got the picture. I will now put a spell on her for you. You must be exact in every detail. You just can't put a spell on somebody unless it is the right person.'

Although we had become quite friendly, simply by the times we had seen each other, his understanding of English culture was still not sufficient for him to understand my humour. He honestly believed I meant what I said.

He walked slowly to the cupboard in the dining room and put on a funny sort of white shirt. As he prepared to put on more regalia I pretended to be somewhat apprehensive.

I said in a very loud voice, 'For God's sake Jimmy, wait a second.'

I put my hand on my brow as he turned to look at me. 'I forgot to tell you Jimmy, but my mother-in-law is a real old witch herself. Is it possible that any spell you put on her might backfire?'

'What do you mean, backfire?' he said.

He was now putting on some funny multicoloured cloak; he had obviously not understood what the expression 'backfire' meant.

'I mean the spell you intend to cast on her will come back to you. I don't know enough about this witchcraft not to ask you this.'

He was struck dumb. I thought that he would have a heart attack there and then. His face turned ashen in colour. He tore off the cloak he was putting on, took off the hat he was wearing, loosened his collar; became breathless and collapsed into a chair.

He refused to carry on. He remained seated. He was adamant. He would not put a curse on my mother-in-law, in spite of all my pleadings. The belief in the supernatural is so great, even in a westernised African, that I had to spend a good deal of time afterwards in reassuring him. He also made me promise I would never in any circumstances mention his name or his existence to my mother-in-law.

I visited Jimmy many times after this episode, but never once did I ever allude to it; neither did he. He went to the grave in 1981 still believing that I was related to a witch!

Jimmy was not the only patient of mine who believed in witchcraft. I had a Nigerian patient of mine in 1974 who told me that she would die in childbirth. The power of the belief in magic and voodoo is such that she had no doubt whatsoever.

A spell had been cast on her back home and she was convinced that no power on earth could save her. She had been told by a witch doctor in Nigeria that she would die in childbirth when her seventh child was born. This pregnancy was her seventh!

I did not have the experience of Jimmy in 1974 and regarded her whole story as stuff and nonsense. How could any sane person living in England in the twentieth century believe such rubbish?

I performed all the routine antenatal examinations through her pregnancy, pooh-poohed all her fears of dying, and sent her into hospital when labour commenced.

She had shown no symptoms of any abnormality during pregnancy and I had no qualms in dismissing her fears. Besides, I had taken the precaution of giving her anti-witch doctor medicine. This, to the uninformed reader, consists of mist. gent. alk. with twenty drops of acetophenatidine added. I have drunk it, it tastes awful. It made me vomit, but it works. I have never been plagued by any witches! No self-respecting witch could possibly come within a mile of anyone drinking this mixture. I was hoping that my pretence in prescribing medicine to combat her fears might have been successful. I was wrong!

To my horror, the midwifery sister of Dulwich Hospital telephoned me after having delivered this lady and said that my patient had been delivered of a normal baby, then died.

She had suffered a cardiac arrest after the delivery, with no prior symptoms. The baby had been born naturally, there had been no complications at the birth and the second stage of labour had lasted one hour. When waiting for the placenta to be delivered, the lady who appeared to be normal, had asked to see the baby. She had been shown a healthy boy, given the baby to hold her in her arms, nursed it for a few minutes, then collapsed. The midwife thought her attack was a simple faint, but it was not, her heart had just stopped beating!

They were unable to resuscitate her. Did I have any suggestions as to what might have caused this lady to have a heart attack? I did not like to be facetious and say the cause of death on the certificate should be voodoo. Nevertheless, after a few seconds hesitation, I remarked that the only answer I could offer was that this lady had a spell put on her in Africa.

I expected a peal of laughter and to my astonishment this did not happen. The maternity sister did not appear to be surprised at what I believed to be a statement of the utmost stupidity. She told me that she had heard of several similar cases to mine of patients who claimed to have been bewitched and died.

Motorbike And Car In Conflict

His father was the rabbi in the South-East London District Synagogue, in New Cross Road, but Daniel Stern, although religious, worshipped speed. Daniel was a young eighteen-year-old tearaway, a heap of fun, but so fearless as to be a positive danger, both to himself and to others. He was adventurous to the extreme. When our cat was stranded at the top of a poplar tree at the bottom of our garden in Brockley, southeast London, in 1964, before sending for the fire brigade we sent for Daniel. He thought it great fun climbing the tree like a monkey and rescuing the animal. The rewards he received from the cat for saving its life were severe scratch marks on the back of his hand and from me - an anti-tetanus injection!

He rode a bicycle and was very proud of the speed he could get up to. Sadly, it was however never fast enough for him to believe that he could kill himself on it. In 1965, when he managed to get a wage rise at his work in the jewellery trade, he bought himself a motorcycle. Now he could travel!

Unfortunately he had been able to buy only a 250 cc bike. His money had stretched only this far; with this he was not too happy. This motorbike was really not fast enough! In 1966 he had another wage rise and gave his motorcycle in part exchange for a 500 cc bike. It was still not fast enough for him. He waited for another pay rise and then bought himself a 1000 cc bike. Now he was happy. This was the bike of his dreams.

What better place to test his new dream purchase than the top of the steep hill in Pepys Road which starts in Avignon Road, Brockley, and dips all the way down to New Cross Road.

The story of one fateful journey of his in 1966 I will never forget. He had actually come to my home in Brockley to chat up our new au pair but, finding her busy, he had been forced to content himself with my company for some time.

'I was coming down the hill in Pepys Road, not too fast, earlier on,' he said, 'when I saw this *old geezer* coming up the hill in a Morris Minor. I thought, "what a smashing way to test the bike." I turned on the throttle; the bike roared smashing like, just like an aeroplane engine. I crossed quickly to the other side of the road, raised the front wheel of the bike, went over the bonnet of the old geezer's car, over the roof, down on to the road, without a scratch. You should have seen the face of the old bloke as I went over his head: I thought his eyes would pop out!'

Incidentally, a lad wearing just a sports shirt and trousers without a helmet performed this feat - head protection was not compulsory at the time.

I only half believed his story. Although I knew he was capable of doing almost anything, I could not believe that he had actually performed this stunt. It was well known that he tended to exaggerate his exploits and I thought this was one of his many exaggerations.

You can imagine my astonishment the following morning, in the surgery, when this 'old geezer', a patient of the ripe old age of forty, came in to see me with this remarkable story.

'You won't believe me! Nobody does. I was minding my own business, driving up Pepys Road, from New Cross Road, early yesterday afternoon, when this mad lunatic came down the hill on a motorbike. He must have been coming down at over 100 miles an hour. This madman suddenly swerved across the road straight at me, climbed over the car bonnet, over the roof, down on to the road without falling off or turning a hair. He must be a raving lunatic, doc. People like him should be locked up!'

Although I had already heard the story, I pretended to be startled. I insinuated that he might be exaggerating, but all he said was that I was like everyone else. No one believed him. He must be going *crackers!* He requested tablets for his nerves. He was beginning to think that he was imagining the whole episode. It was all a dream. Nothing had happened. He had *flipped!* I now suggested to him that if his story were true the motorbike must have damaged his car. His answer was a pointed - 'No!'

The bike was going so fast that it had run over the car as if the car was the road itself. He had seen the same trick done at a circus by a stunt rider but never believed - until yesterday - that it was possible to do the same thing on a normal road. He had not been able to stop shaking since the incident. He had not been able to sleep. His wife had persuaded him to come to see me instead of going to work.

I certainly did not divulge that I knew the story to be true, but asked him where his car was now parked.

'It's outside,' he said.

I suggested that if we went outside to look for any damage we would almost certainly find a small scratch or indentation. The incident had happened only the previous day, and the motorcycle tyres must have been in contact with the car at some point. It was just not possible for a bike to have been airborne all the time. It must have touched the car at some point to have been able to go over the top. He would not have felt it; he would have been too shocked. We had to find something if he were telling the truth.

He looked crestfallen but reluctantly agreed. We went on our tour of inspection and when I pointed out to him a small scratch on the bonnet, and a small dent in the roof, he became wild with excitement. Someone believed his story! The incident had actually happened! I could see the relief on his face. He was so relieved he suddenly flung his arms around me and kissed me.

Spinster Avoided Examination

My relationship with Miss Woods who lived in Hillcourt Road, East Dulwich, in the 'sixties, was ill defined from our first meeting. She was a fifty-year-old spinster who became my patient not by recommendation but through politics. Hillcourt Road was nowhere near my surgery - there were many doctors between her residence and my surgery premises - but these doctors had not signed on the British Medical Association's scheme's list of private practitioners.

In the '60s the BMA, in its usual tussle with the government over the management of the National Health Service, decided to set up a rival scheme for general practitioners. General practitioners were invited to join an agency, which would run the scheme, and patients were invited to pay the agency five shillings a month. Unfortunately, so few doctors and patients joined, the scheme was short-lived. The few patients assigned to me left - except for Miss Woods.

The reason why she remained as my patient was that she was bedridden. I am afraid I never ever found out what caused this tragedy. She simply refused to discuss it, and would only admit being treated once only by a doctor, before she signed up with the agency. I was given to understand on my first visit to her that any physical examination was to be kept to the minimum and she was not to be questioned as to her past history or employment. She admitted that she had a present occupation; this was translating Polish documents into English, and English documents into Polish. She admitted to me that she could not speak Polish, but as a religious person, felt it her duty to support the persecuted Polish religious movement in freeing itself from Russian occupation. She appeared to have no family and was cared for by a Polish friend who lived opposite her, in the same road. This friend was, in my opinion, a member of the Polish underground movement for the translations on the bed were always related to Lech Walensa. In my limited knowledge of the Polish underground movement - from the media - he was the head of it.

Miss Woods told me on many occasions that she did not believe in the NHS and that is why she registered with the agency. On its collapse, she said that she would continue to pay me five shillings a month for my services and I foolishly accepted the agreement. Unfortunately I was often out of pocket but I did not have the heart nor will to ask her to take her services elsewhere.

She was a tyrant and would brook no contradiction. It was not a normal doctor patient relationship. She ordered; I obeyed. She would allow no examination below the waist. When she had a cough, and examination of her chest was required, my stethoscope had to be manipulated under her nightdress. I saw her only in a nightdress; and dressing gown when it was cold. For heat, in the winter, there was a paraffin stove under the window. This produced such obnoxious fumes that on occasions I felt nauseous and had to stifle the feeling to vomit. I would never have had the audacity to ask her to trim the wick for fear that she would have asked me to do it. Interestingly, when on one occasion I plucked up courage to ask her about the pock marks on her neck and arms she admitted that she had been in a fever hospital for some months in 1928, when a child, suffering from smallpox. She is the only patient in my experience of over fifty years in general practice that I have seen who had smallpox.

I was never allowed to examine her legs or feet until her final illness; this was over twenty years after our first meeting. Why was I required to attend her? To confirm monthly the diagnosis of Hiatus Hernia, made by a doctor whose name she was not prepared to give me, and to prescribe a bottle of Mist Kaolin Sed. My examination consisted of prodding her abdomen, in the umbilical area, over her nightdress and bed jacket.

For recreation, she wrote letters to the press about local conditions and political matters. It was interesting to read some of her letters - printed in the winter in the local press - about conditions on the pavements where the snow had not been cleared. She had not left her bed! She was an educated lady who spoke French fluently. She was so reticent in discussing her past life, that however hard I tried, I never found out what had made her take to her bed and how she managed to prolong it without becoming bored.

She received a pension, but never told me from whom or what her relationship was to Poland and the Poles with whom she was in contact. My curiosity was aroused on many occasions when Poland was a news item and she had Polish papers lying all over her bed. Her only reaction to any enquiry was that her Polish friend opposite had dropped in the papers and she was writing a letter for her.

Her friend, who lived in a house on the opposite side of the road, was a Polish lady whose accent was so unmistakeable that I recognised it the first time I met her. It was so much like that of my father-in-law. I thought they came from the same town until she told me that to an Englishman all Polish dialects sounded the same. The friend worked for a government department and earned enough to run a car.

This car became a topic of conversation on many occasions. She never worked weekends. She parked her car outside her house on Friday evening, and found when she came to use it on Saturday morning, it did not appear to have moved. She always filled the petrol tank on her way home on Friday evening but the surprise was, it was now half empty. The mileage too had increased. Someone obviously had a key to her car and had used it without permission.

In the early hours one Saturday morning she had looked out of her window and found the car was missing. She telephoned East Dulwich Police Station in Lordship Lane to report the loss and they promised to send someone to take particulars. When they came, the car was in its usual position. She was reprimanded and warned about wasting police time! She told them that she believed it was her neighbour who took it to visit his girlfriend when his wife went to spend the weekend with her mother. She was furious when one of the officers told her that if she repeated this, and was killed by her neighbour, the police would believe that her death had been a natural one! The other police officer had suggested that she ask the neighbour for the cost of the petrol. They obviously believed that she was a cantankerous old spinster wanting to make trouble and involve herself in matters that were not of her concern.

To prove the police were wrong, she spent the next three weeks in watch all Friday night, from her upstairs bedroom, with her eyes glued on the car. It never moved! Neither did the speedometer reading. The following week, on Saturday morning, she came down and when she went to her car found that the speedometer reading had increased by two hundred miles. She could not believe her eyes. She could only postulate that she had fallen asleep during her night's watch. She had read the speedometer on Friday night; there could be no mistake! Without hesitation, she drove the car to the police station in Lordship Lane, to be confronted by the same officer who had dealt with her previous complaint. He was polite and suggested that one of her neighbours must be the culprit and that she should employ a private detective agency to investigate and substantiate her claim. Alternatively, if she knew Denmark Hill, there was a hospital there called the Maudsley that dealt with problems from which she was suffering. Should she reappear at the police station without taking his advice he might have to charge her and she would have to appear before magistrates for wasting police time. My distress on learning from Miss Woods that the lady had moved to Tring before I found out the results of the confrontation can only be imagined!

I realised at my first consultation with Miss Woods that our relationship was to be a superficial one. She needed a doctor to give her medical certificates and prescriptions, not give her any advice. He was there as her servant. She believed in private medicine. Not having the means to employ a doctor who worked in the private sector she had jumped at the opportunity the BMA had given her.

I examined Miss Woods one morning during one of my routine monthly visits and, as usual, was not allowed to remove her bed jacket. In the evening, I was asked to make an emergency call by one of her social workers as she had found her bed jacket coated with blood. Miss Woods had not asked for the visit, but the social worker was worried. She knew that I had a key to the flat, so requested that I call on my way home from the surgery. On this occasion, in spite of Miss Wood's objections, I insisted on removing her bed jacket and clothes above the waist. I was startled to find a massive cancer of the breast, which she admitted she had successfully hidden from me for years.

I arranged her immediate admission to hospital. She even argued with me over the admission. She agreed only when I told her that my visits to her had now ended unless she did as she was told. Treated by the hospital and Macmillan nurses, her life was extended for 20 months.

May her dear soul rest in peace.

Morbid Tale

It is a custom of many tribes to arrange their own funerals before they die. Tribal chiefs are always buried according to their traditional beliefs. One can arrange in some parts of America to have one's body deep-frozen, until scientists achieve the ultimate and bring the body back to life. The Pyramids and Taj Mahal are memorials to man's enterprise in perpetuating the memory of the dead. The Cave of Machpelloh in Hebron is mentioned in the Old Testament as having been bought by Abraham from Ephrom the Hittite for four hundred shekels as a burying place for his wife, Sarah. This is cited as proof of the relationship of the Israelites to Israel. It was a freehold purchase!

Burials and memorials are never far from a doctor's life, but I was surprised when Mrs Lawrence told me in 1988 that she had booked her own funeral and wanted my approval. She did not want to burden her son who now had a family of his own to worry about.

As she was only sixty-eight years old, I wondered whether she was telling me what a failure I was as a doctor, that she had seen another practitioner, and I had missed a diagnosis. Was she using this method of reproach by telling me to be more perceptive in the future? Perhaps she had been to a clairvoyant who had foretold her future. Had she been told what a lousy doctor I was in not sending her to a consultant who might have prolonged her life?

I made no remark. I just grinned as she continued the conversation. The cost was going to be eight hundred pounds. I winced. She continued saying it was going to be the funeral of her dreams. She had chosen the coffin. It was to be cream wood, varnished, and lined with lemon padded silk. Did I know, she remarked, that some undertakers used materials that were rough on the skin. I smiled a sickly grin and asked, 'why the padding?' She answered without blinking. 'I took the undertaker's advice; he said thick padding would save me a bumpy ride.'

Coffins, she explained, came in all sizes and shapes. She had heard of one body that had been too long for the coffin, and had to be doubled up to fit. A coffin had to be wide enough too - if one wanted space enough to breathe. There was nothing worse than being in an uncomfortable coffin lying there in it for eternity.

I listened to her spellbound. At first I thought that she was pulling my leg but there was not a hint of facetiousness in her remarks. She meant every word she said. The undertaker was certainly an excellent salesman: he deserved every bit of credit for his powers of persuasion.

He told her the price of the performance was a bargain. It was a set price and included VAT. With rising inflation, she was making an excellent investment. There were unfortunately one or two snags. The funeral directors had made the transaction non-transferable. It was exclusive to her body. Should she die abroad, she would lose her money. She had to die in the United Kingdom. Since the burial was to take place in Honor Oak Crematorium, the undertakers had agreed to bring her body back from anywhere outside London - at no extra cost!

I still made no comment. Not only had the salesman been able to persuade her to buy a superior coffin, he had had the *chutzpah* to make her believe she was to lie in her coffin for eternity - after having been cremated!

She had paid cash down. She would be allowed two cars for the mourners, apart from the hearse. To make sure she had the perfect funeral, she had also given a sum of money to her son for extra cars should they be needed. She had many friends and was sure the extra money would be needed. Most of her friends were old and did not have cars of their own. She had given the receipt from the undertakers to her son for safekeeping so there would be no problems. All was now ready for the great send off. She actually said she was looking forward to it.

I listened to the whole story completely mystified and confused.

Perhaps I am morbid but her enthusiasm rather escaped me!

———

Surrounded By Lovely
Imaginary Girls

Mr Warrener, a patient of mine from the day I commenced in practice in Peckham, had an arrangement with Mr Deveson the landlord of the Hope public house in Rye Lane. Mr Warrener was the bookie's runner, who took bets every day in that establishment. My story relates to the period in 1955, when everyone knew that Mr Warrener's work was illegal. He also took bets while standing in a telephone kiosk, or standing on a street corner in Rye Lane. This discipline was for people who did not frequent public hostelry and needed to use his services. His function was to take the betting slips with the punters' money, carry them to the local bookmaker's office and pay out the lucky winners on the following day, in the same illegal fashion.

Obviously his favourite place of business was the Hope Pub. Here the punters would buy him drinks; the landlord too was friendly as it was good for trade. A person coming in to place a bet invariably bought a drink and, if lucky afterwards, made sure he spent a good deal of his winnings in the friendly atmosphere of the warm establishment.

Mr Warrener was well known to the police, but they mostly turned a blind eye to his dealings. When it was time for the police to make an arrest for betting, they informed him of the fact - to give him time to find a stooge. The stooge, paid by the bookie to play the part of the 'runner', would be arrested. Not having been previously involved in this illegal activity, the stooge appeared before the magistrate as a first offender, and would receive only a ten-pound fine. This the bookie would pay and the stooge would be rewarded handsomely for his stand-in part. Mr Warrener - having already been apprehended several times by over-zealous policemen - would have been labelled a frequent offender and have received a much heavier fine - even a custodial sentence. Because of his trade, he spent most of his life in public houses and he was my first encounter with the DTs (delirium tremens).

I was called to see him late one night, in November 1956, when he was living in Fenwick Road. He was running a high temperature, shivering and hallucinating - and had taken to his bed. He had a persistent cough. His sputum was rust coloured. After I examined his chest there was no doubt in my mind that this poor fellow had acute lobar pneumonia.

I gave him an injection of penicillin and told the lady who was nursing him that I would call again the following morning before I began my surgery, to give him another injection. I told her that if she was at all concerned during the night she should send for me and I would send him into hospital. I was quite happy with his nursing care; the lady attending him was a neighbour of mine in Bellenden Road.

On the following morning, when I called to give him a second injection, he recognised me, greeted me and sat up in bed. With staring hollow eyes he then insisted that I raise the hat I was wearing to the lovely girls Beryl, Sybil, Frances, Marilyn, Dulcie and Cheryl, who were in various parts of his room. I looked at him speechless. I thought he was joking. There were only two people in the room! He certainly was not joking! When he saw that I was not making any great haste in complying with his request, he began to shout at me for not behaving like a gentleman. He became hysterical. He tried to get out of bed with the obvious intention of striking me. I did not wait to be asked again. I felt like a blithering idiot as I raised my trilby hat to these imaginary ladies. It was not the raising of my hat that made me feel so foolish, I was wondering whether I had made the wrong diagnosis on the previous night and that Mr Warrener had gone mad. I had never previously seen a patient with the DTs.

He shouted that two girls were sitting on his wardrobe and I had not taken any notice of them. He appeared very irritated! One of them was apparently attempting to climb out of his open upstairs window and he was shouting at her not to do so. My concern was - in attempting to save her - he might climb out of bed and I would be left having to drag a heavy maniac back. I might even be unsuccessful. He might in his panic-stricken state fall out of the window. To humour him, I ran to the wardrobe, grabbed an imaginary pair of ankles and pulled them down. I performed an imaginary rescue of the girl. I have never felt such a fool in my whole life! I have never been much of an actor but I certainly played an excellent part that morning. I fooled him. I now went to the window and closed it firmly with the excuse that it was impossible to examine anybody in such a cold room.

Suddenly without warning, as I was examining his chest, he pushed me aside to sweep away the imaginary spiders on his bed. When I recommenced my examination he told me that his cat had just jumped on his bed and he now kept stroking a fantasy cat. It cost me a good deal of patience and time treating this fellow. Trying to give a patient an injection in his arm when he suddenly decides to use his arm to push away a cat, which is attempting to scratch his face, is no joke. After the injection, he insisted his room had become full of cats. He attempted to get out of bed. The district nurse had now arrived and we had the farcical situation of a qualified doctor and a qualified nurse, shooing non-existent cats from his room. Anyone passing by would have had us locked up as *loonies!* Surprisingly, he never complained that there were mice or rats in his room. I had always been taught that a person who suffers from Delirium Tremens always sees imaginary rodents. Perhaps the cats had driven them away! I left him that morning in a dishevelled state and wondered what further excitement awaited me when I did repeat visits.

The performance of raising my hat to his imaginary girls persisted on my visits to him that evening and on the following morning, but I benefited by not having to make any rescue attempts. It had however reached the stage when I seriously considered breaking my tradition and leaving my trilby hat in the car. I had solved the window problem by closing it firmly, it could not be opened easily. I wondered what other tests he would set me if I appeared in his room hatless. I never tempted the fates. I went to see him on every occasion with my hat perched firmly on my head so that we could play out our little charade.

I visited him twice daily to give him penicillin injections and monitor his progress. Happily, the penicillin worked quickly. His temperature dropped after the fourth injection and his cough improved. I arranged for the district nurse to attend once daily in the morning to give some respite to the lady who was caring for him and to provide some general nursing care. Unfortunately, although he appeared much better physically, his delusions still continued, until I managed to persuade the nurse that not only was penicillin necessary for Mr Warrener's recovery so too was a pint of Guinness.

On my instructions, on the fourth day, he was given a pint of Guinness. The result was miraculous! When I returned that evening he behaved normally. No mention was made of girls, cats, spiders or other fictitious characters in his room. He recovered completely. He lived another twenty years, until in his seventies, when he had another bout of pneumonia. This was so virulent he survived only one day. This attack did not even give him time to mention cats, spiders, or 'those lovely girls on top of the wardrobe'.

———————

What A Bingo Win!

Patrick and Nancy Fitzpatrick were the lucky pair who had won a prize - the top prize in the Top Rank Bingo Club. It was 1977, and the prize was a trip for two to Monte Carlo! Every one of my patients who knew of this lucky win was envious. It was not surprising. Who would not be green with envy over a couple who struck so lucky with such good fortune just by playing bingo?

Mr Patrick Fitzpatrick worked for a firm of contractors as a sprinkler fitter, fitting sprinklers in large buildings for use in case of fire. However hard he worked, he had never earned enough to be able to afford a trip such as this, with hotel and all expenses paid. His work demanded that he travel the length and breadth of this country but never abroad. He had worked in an airport at odd times for over twenty years installing sprinklers in the shops and new hangars, but the only occasion he had left these shores was on a trip to Ireland - and this was by boat. He had never flown. He had never been inside an aircraft. The thought of being in the air terrified him.

We now had a problem. The prize, a week in Monte Carlo, included the airfare. Although the couple were overjoyed at their good fortune, Patrick spent sleepless nights worrying about the journey. Mrs Fitzpatrick did not have the same worry. She had flown before. She had been on pilgrimages to Lourdes and the travel had always been by air.

Patrick was persuaded both by his wife and me that he had nothing to worry about. He was a religious man. He never missed going to church every Sunday. The prize had obviously been given as a gift from heaven. Our persuasive powers overcame his reluctance. He duly arrived at the airport terminal at the appointed time and took his seat on the aircraft.

The plane took off at its appointed time and the flight was uneventful until they reached Nice. The few hours that they had travelled had by this time made Patrick feel that his fears of flying had been unfounded. He was now glad that he had agreed to go. The plane had met no turbulence; the flight had been so smooth he could not feel the plane was actually in motion. The food on the flight was good and drink was plentiful. The airhostesses were pretty and helpful. The girls were actually making a fuss of him. He was enjoying himself.

Suddenly, over Nice, just a few miles from their destination, the plane fell 12,000 feet, and became depressurised. It had fallen out of the sky without warning or meeting any turbulence.

There was panic on the plane. Mrs Nancy Fitzpatrick, a religious Catholic, was not to be distressed by what God had in store for her. She calmly stood up and taking out the holy water from her handbag, proceeded to make blessings as she walked down the gangway sprinkling the water on the passengers. Patrick meanwhile had collapsed in his seat. She had taken no notice of him. She knew his fear of flying. She thought he was suffering from shock. Even though he lay prostrate in his seat she continued her religious ministrations.

In the meantime the plane had righted itself. They were told that one of the engines of the plane had failed, but there was no danger, and the plane would be returning to Luton rather than being stranded in Monte Carlo. On review, Patrick's collapse was not only due to shock, but he had also suffered his first mild CVA (stroke).

The plane, in order to avoid being stranded in Monte Carlo and having to pay expensive airport fees before being repaired, limped back to Luton where it made an emergency landing. The passengers were then offered another flight to Monte Carlo, but Patrick and Nancy refused the offer. They had suffered enough! No amount of persuasion on behalf of the airline could make them board another plane, even though all the other passengers did so. They returned home.

Poor Mr Fitzpatrick was in bed for six weeks after his return. He was unable to swallow properly, lost two stones in weight and, to be honest, was never right until he departed this life. He recovered enough after a few months' convalescence to stagger back to work, but managed to do so only until 1981 when he had another stroke. It was only a small one but was followed by several more similar strokes. Although he appeared to recover physically afterwards, each one left him a little more mentally disturbed. After each stroke he became more neurotic and more of a hypochondriac, which took up a lot more of my time in treating his symptoms.

It appears to be a fact of life that misfortune, illness, or conversely luck, once it appears, continues to strike the same person over and over again. Misfortune having once shown its ugly face certainly continued to dog poor Patrick. He bought a bottle of his favourite beer one day, put it down by the side of his favourite chair, then it exploded and injured him. He claimed against the company and his claim was not contested. The claim was settled out of court - they must have heard of Patrick's luck!

This injury deepened Patrick's depression. He had never been the same since his flight to Monte Carlo and the bottle injury made him feel that he should do nothing. He stayed in bed most of the day; Nancy could now get him out of bed for only ten minutes, to take the dog for a walk.

However hard she tried - this would be only once a day - he came home complaining that he was tired and exhausted. He was unable to concentrate for any length of time, completely lacked motivation, and became more of a hypochondriac as each day passed.

He got up for breakfast and after eating it, went back to bed. He got up for lunch at 12.30 p.m., ate it and went back to bed again. Tea was the only exception to the routine. He got up for tea at 4.30 p.m., but instead of returning to bed he took the dog for its ten minute walk. He then went to bed! He got up again at 8 p.m., had his supper, and went to bed. This routine was followed day after day. He had become a walking cabbage!

The same cycle continued for a whole year before I was able to persuade the Fitzpatricks that my knowledge of treating a man with these symptoms was minimal. They had the wrong doctor for his complaint! With his symptoms, psychiatric help was indicated. It still however took a good deal of persuasion on my part before they agreed to do so. He saw a psychiatrist, who arranged sessions for him for a number of years. The only help we received from him was that Patrick left his bed when he had an appointment to see him! His help was minimal.

His last visit to the psychiatrist was in November 1990 when the psychiatrist explained that due to the problems with the hospital budget it was now unable to meet its commitments. It was forced to cut down on its outpatient clinics and now accepted only emergency referrals. Patrick had in any event been attending only for social reasons - somewhere to go after being confined to the house all day long, looking at the walls. For some time, improvement in his symptoms had been minimal. Patrick knew that the psychiatrist was aware of this.

He therefore understood the implications of the psychiatrist's remarks when he said, 'we have been unable to do very much for you Mr Fitzpatrick, in all the years that we have been treating you. Perhaps your GP would have been just as good.'

Patrick did not answer.

The psychiatrist then looked into his eyes and without batting an eyelid said, '*Have you ever contemplated suicide?*'

'Not until you just mentioned it,' he replied.

As my relationship with Patrick had extended for over thirty-five years, I was left having to cope with Patrick until the Good Lord decided to take him into his keeping.

The moral of this story is, if 'you have to win at bingo for God's sake don't win the top prize!'

Amazing Hat Trick Of Deaths

It was a lovely warm sunny May morning in 1962 when I was asked to visit Mr Raymond Wellington in Copleston Road. The reason given for the request was that he was not feeling too well, not ill enough to go to bed, but not well enough to come to the surgery. He was short of breath, suffering from indigestion, felt sick and had vomited twice. The message as passed to me also gave the diagnosis - he had eaten a ham sandwich for breakfast and it had upset his stomach. The visit I was informed was not urgent; it could wait until after the morning surgery.

I was already attending the Wellington sisters and three of the brothers with their various complaints; it could be said that I knew the family very well. It was a strange family. There were seven Wellingtons in all - four brothers and three sisters. Three brothers and three sisters, all in their late fifties or early sixties and all unmarried, lived in the same house in Copleston Road. The seventh brother, the eldest, was the exception. He was married, lived in a Kent village and was the only member of the family who was not a patient of mine.

The brother to whom I had been called had a history of heart trouble. He had suffered from rheumatic fever as a child. This had damaged his heart but he had never had a heart attack. The technology we have today was not available in 1962 so the severity of his heart disease had been impossible to evaluate.

Raymond was a short stocky man aged fifty-eight. When I arrived at the house at 11.30 a.m. on that sunny morning he was sitting in an armchair in the lounge with his right arm firmly clutching his breastbone. He complained of a feeling of tightness in his chest like a tight band. He could not stop belching. He gave me the diagnosis - indigestion. As he was talking to me, telling me his symptoms, his face became ashen: his lips became white and he began fighting for his breath. He head fell forward. He collapsed in the chair, lost consciousness and fell off it. I made every effort to resuscitate him. I even gave him an injection of adrenaline into his heart but it was useless. A post mortem later revealed that he had suffered a massive heart attack.

I called an ambulance. When the attendants found that the fellow was dead, and I was prepared to sign the death certificate, they refused to take the body away. They were allowed to take only live bodies away not dead ones, they said.

I packed my medical bag, told the sisters to contact Mays, the local undertakers in Rye Lane, and prepared to leave. I told them they should tell the undertakers that I would be willing to sign the death certificate as I had attended Raymond before he had died. The cause of death was coronary thrombosis. I still had other patients to visit so I said that if one of the sisters came to the surgery later on - after I had completed my visits - I would give her the certificate to take to the registrar. His offices, I explained, were situated opposite the Town Hall in Peckham Road.

One of the sisters then asked whether, before leaving, I could spare the time to have a look at James who was in the upstairs bedroom, not feeling too well. He had been in the lounge when I arrived, but had disappeared when his brother had collapsed. The sister told me that he had become distressed on hearing of his brother's death and had collapsed on the bed. I did not wait to hear any more. I ran up the stairs like a hare. I was already too late. He was laying face upwards on the bed, completely lifeless. His lips were deep purple and frothy blood was slowly oozing from the side of his mouth. He had obviously been dead for some minutes. There was nothing I could do.

To say this double tragedy shocked me would be an understatement. I went down the stairs with two of the sisters numbed and shattered. I had never had two deaths in the same house, at the same time, before. Thank heavens, in my fifty years in general practice this has not been repeated.

I sat with the three sisters in the back kitchen-cum-dining room for some minutes discussing what was best to do in this extraordinary situation. Now that two brothers had decided to depart on the same day, in the same house, in what appeared to be the same fashion, I suggested that it would be best for me to refer both deaths to the coroner. They would not listen. I had treated both brothers previously for heart trouble. It would save them a good deal of aggravation and pain if I issued death certificates.

'After all, you have been treating both of them for some years for heart trouble,' said one of the sisters. 'Ask Harold, he will tell you how ill they were!'

Harold was the third brother in the house. He had gone to the toilet on my arrival. I had now been in the house for over an hour. We all suddenly looked at one another, stunned into silence. There were four of us in that room but no Harold.

The three sisters, for the one and only time, looked as if their world had collapsed. Indeed, it already had! The eldest sister was fat, round-faced, rosy-cheeked, staid and unflappable. The second sister, the youngest, was taller, very much thinner and suffered from multiple sclerosis. She was only able to get about in a wheelchair, then with difficulty. She had remained downstairs when we had the problem of the second brother's demise. The loss of the two brothers had not affected her as much emotionally as the other sisters. This presumably was due to the fact she had seen only one dead brother. The third sister, of medium height, thin-faced and who never smiled, was a multi-symptomatic lady.

She was in a state of constant anxiety, a complete bag of nerves; her hands shook all the time. She came to see me in the surgery every couple of days with a new symptom. I had not as yet found anything organically wrong with her. I believe she would have been happier had I done so. Nevertheless, we had a friendly relationship. Even though she complained that my treatment had not cured her of her symptoms she bore me no malice. She obviously did not want to be cured. She enjoyed living with, what she believed to be, ill health.

Their home in Copleston Road was an old rambling three-storey house. As I had seen Harold only once since coming into it I naturally thought he had gone to the toilet. I asked no questions. I ran through the kitchen, round the back of the house to the toilet. The door was open. The toilet was empty and Harold was not there.

I walked back into the dining room looking puzzled. I asked them if Harold could possibly have gone out.

'He has gone to the toilet,' they answered in unison.

'I have just looked, he is not there;' I answered.

'We had an inside toilet and bathroom put in upstairs only a few weeks ago, he must have gone there,' they said.

I ran upstairs. I tried the toilet door. It was locked. I shouted, 'Harold! Harold!'

There was no answer.

The two sisters who were mobile had by this time joined me upstairs, but the fat one had joined me in such a state of breathlessness that I thought more resuscitation was going to be required. I began to bang on the toilet door. As this brought no response from the occupant, I put my ear to the door to see whether I could hear movement. I could hear nothing. I then asked the ladies whether I could have permission to force the lock.

The unflappable sister, the one who was always in charge and did all the housekeeping, had by this time recovered from her climb up the stairs. She now appeared as composed as ever and gave her permission.

I broke the door down with a heavy chair. Poor Harold was sitting on the toilet - lifeless. His head was bent forward on his chest; his corpulent body had prevented him from falling off the *throne*.

I could not believe it. My head swam. I was losing so many patients at such a fast rate that if it continued at this pace I would have no practice left in three days! The two sisters who had followed me up the stairs did not appear at that time as shaken as I was. I had indeed treated all three brothers for heart trouble - they were not youngsters - but to lose all three in one day was not a very good way of building up a flourishing practice and a reputation.

The three sisters seemed to take the whole ghastly business in their stride. Even the multi-symptomatic lady - who spent her whole life moaning and groaning - did not appear too upset. The youngest sister in the wheelchair, when we came downstairs and broke the news to her, simply looked at me and remarked!

'Can you arrange to have our brothers taken away before it gets dark?'

She apparently did not like to have dead bodies in the house after nightfall! Of the group who had avoided death in that house in Copleston Road that morning I appeared to be the most upset. In retrospect, it must have been because I was in my thirties; they were in the sixties, with far more experience of life and its vagaries.

While feeling sorry for the sisters who had lost three brothers on the same day this amazing experience does not give one's practice a very good name. Patients are very reluctant to register with a doctor who appears to specialise in death, especially if he is in the wholesale business. It has to be remembered that I am writing of an event which took place forty years before Dr Shipman entered the wholesale business!

The coroner's officer, to whom I reported the deaths, listened to me in stony silence as I rattled off the names one after the other. He retorted that it did seem rather unusual to have three deaths in one house at the same time. I told him that my diagnosis for every one of the departures was coronary thrombosis. I had been treating each of the brothers for heart trouble for some time. I did not suspect anything unusual to be the cause of the deaths.

'What did they all have for breakfast?' he asked.

I was stumped. I had to admit that I had not asked.

'Well, they could all have been poisoned you know!' he suggested.

I felt a real fool. It had not crossed my mind at the time.

He told me not to worry; he would deal with the problem. I should leave everything to him he said. He then rather punctiliously corrected himself: he would deal with the 'problems.' He would let me know the result of his findings in due course.

Post mortems performed on the three brothers proved that I was correct in only two of my diagnoses; the brother who had collapsed on the toilet had suffered a massive cerebrovascular accident.

The three sisters afterwards went on with their lives as if nothing untoward had happened. The multi-symptomatic sister continued to drive me mad with her various complaints until she died a few years later of bronchopneumonia.

The fat sister suffered a stroke in her seventies and died in St. Francis Hospital, East Dulwich.

The youngest sister, the one who suffered from multiple sclerosis, had to be admitted to a special home when her fat sister had a stroke. There was no one left at home to care for her. I am afraid I lost contact with her after her admission

———————

Mrs Eubanks

My practice had increased so rapidly by 1961 that I decided to try out an appointment system and add a bit of prestige by employing a receptionist. For this purpose as my first receptionist I engaged Mrs Ellen O'Brien - a patient and an ex-nurse who had been forced to give up nursing to cope with her two young children.

She worked for me part-time, but had previously been a staff nurse at King's College Hospital, trained in midwifery by Mrs Pretty who had been a sister tutor there.

As Mrs Pretty was a patient of mine it always amused me when she came in to see me. Mrs O'Brien could not forget that she was no longer her pupil. She bowed and scraped before sister tutor and always addressed her as Madam; after she left she called her 'Sister Pee'.

One of my Jamaican patients, Mrs Eubanks, who had arrived in this country in 1960 appeared to spend her life feuding with Mrs O'Brien. Mrs Eubanks called me out for visits to her children on the slightest pretext and had a turn of phrase which always amused me. If one of her children was missing, not to be found easily, she would shout, 'Where you is?' When the child appeared her raucous voice bellowed out, 'Where you was?'

I tried as hard as I could to persuade the lady to bring her children to the surgery; it was a useless exercise. Her mind could not absorb the reason for an appointment system. She had always managed to see me for her illnesses by gate crashing; she could see no reason for change. The appointment system was in its infancy and Mrs O'Brien had tried, without success, to make Mrs Eubanks understand that in order to see the doctor an appointment had to be made. Mrs Eubanks however cared nothing for Mrs O'Brien - or for appointments.

The day arrived, when for some unknown reason, Mrs Eubanks decided to make an appointment and Mrs O'Brien had managed to give her an appointment for the same day, on a cancellation. She kept the appointment but on leaving me after the consultation she frightened the life out of me. She told me that she had just had enough of that bitch at the desk and was going to punch that filthy German bitch in the mouth. The trouble was she meant it! She was a five foot nine inch eighteen stone woman and almost certainly packed a hefty punch. I pretended to be astonished.

' You don't know what you are talking about or you wouldn't say such things,' I said.

'Do you know who Mrs O'Brien is?'

I explained that it would be the most foolish thing in the world even to attempt to punch my receptionist. Mrs O'Brien was not German, as she believed, but Irish and one of the leaders of the IRA in this country. It was obvious Mrs Eubanks knew nothing about the Irish; if she did, she would have known that it would have been foolish to row with my receptionist. Should Mrs O'Brien be attacked she would have no hesitation in taking out the gun she kept in her handbag and Mrs Eubanks would end up dead! Mrs Eubanks must have realised by now, I continued, that I myself was scared of my receptionist. The IRA had forced my receptionist on to me. Mrs Eubanks should remember that I had worked quite successfully without a receptionist before Mrs O'Brien came!

'What would you do if a gun was held to your head? If you still intend to punch her' - here I emphasized my remark by opening one of the drawers in my desk and taking out the book of death certificates - 'it will save us both a lot of time if I give you a certificate now.'

Mrs Eubanks turned an ashen colour. She had obviously heard about the IRA. What I had said, and the serious face which I had put on specially for the occasion, had frightened her. She turned and left me without saying another word. She was determined to get away from the surgery as quickly as possible.

I silently followed her. I was curious to see what would happen when she actually came face to face with 'one of the leaders of the IRA' when she passed reception. My curiosity was rewarded. As she came down the passage towards reception she went down on to her knees, flattened out her bulky body, and crawled towards the front door like a woodlouse. She was going to make sure that she was below the level of the reception desk, out of the view of the deadly Ellen the 'crack shot' of the IRA.

Even though I had frightened her out of her wits, she still remained one of my patients, but was now studiously polite to Mrs O'Brien. My concern had been, when she told me that she intended to flatten my poor receptionist, that she had a mental history and she had at one time had treatment in Jamaica.

It therefore came as no surprise when she had a nervous breakdown in 1967. She became so disturbed that I referred her to Dr Isaacs, the psychiatrist at St Giles' Hospital, for treatment. Although her treatment was now no longer my responsibility I became involved one sunny afternoon when I was called to the hospital to sort out a problem. She had been due to see Dr Isaacs on the previous day but for some reason had missed her appointment. With her inborn hatred of receptionists, she had proceeded to have a slanging match with the psychiatric receptionist at not being given an appointment for that same day at a time convenient to Mrs Eubanks. The receptionist had stood her ground and had given her an appointment for the following day. This was just not good enough for Mrs Eubanks.

Thwarted by the receptionist, she fled into the hospital grounds and began to throw stones at the ward windows. She had already broken a few windows and no one -sensibly - was prepared to approach a tall, muscular, eighteen stone mad woman, armed with a handful of stones. The psychiatric department had determined by this time that there was only one way to deal with this menace – to have her sectioned and admitted to a mental hospital.

The Mental Health Act stated that two doctors and a social worker were required to sign away her freedom. One doctor had to be her own general practitioner, a person who knew her and would recognise that her behaviour was abnormal. I had therefore been sent for on this lovely sunny day to sign the first part of the compulsory section order for her to be detained.

Fortunately I had always had a rapport with Mrs Eubanks. When she saw me approaching, she put her arm down and stopped throwing. She still however had a handful of stones. I was careful not to get too close. Mentally ill people can behave abnormally! I shouted to her from a distance that her stone throwing was never going to obtain the required results. It was a useless exercise.

She waved to me to come closer and for ten minutes I became a stupid hero. I went up close to her and explained that she obviously did not have the strength to break more windows. The unbroken ones were now too high and at too great a distance. If she would allow me to give her one of my muscle-strengthening injections she would be able to reach the top easily. She trusted me implicitly. She gave me her bare left arm. I gave her an injection of largactil – three times the normal dose.

It still took ten minutes of continuous talking before her responses became slower and she became too drowsy to answer me. She lay down, curled herself into a ball and began to snore. The two ambulance attendants almost ruptured themselves in lifting her on to a stretcher to remove her!

Cigarette Caused Death By Fire

Mrs Nurse owned a flower shop in the '70s in Peckham Rye, almost opposite the large Co-operative store that stood close to the junction of Rye Lane and Heaton Road. She became a private patient of mine in 1972. At that time for me to have a private patient in Peckham was like finding a pot of gold. She was a descendant of a long line of flower sellers; her family had been in the trade for generations. As the family had lived in the area the business was well known and established. Mrs Nurse's main work was making wreaths, sheaves and wedding bouquets. I used to watch her as she wove greenery and flowers in wire frames with her nimble fingers. She continued talking to me and describing her symptoms so she didn't waste time and lose concentration. The end result of her work showed that her concentration had not been affected by my visits. Incidentally, this establishment made my daughter's wedding bouquet and also provided flowers for the *chupah* in the South East London Synagogue.

At my daughter's wedding I persuaded Mr Michael O'Shea, a patient and a devout Catholic who played the organ in the local Catholic Church, to play the organ in the synagogue. I believe I pacified his conscience and overcame his reluctance by informing him that Dr and Mrs Healy - both well-known as devout co-religionists - would also be at the ceremony. He was sufficiently reassured by their presence that he would not be rewarded with eternal damnation for his synagogue performance!

I first became acquainted with Mrs Nurse when she was over seventy years of age after she had already been ill for some years. She was dissatisfied with her previous doctor's treatment. Her niece, who had been a National Health patient of mine for some years, had recommended me to her. The problem was that the old lady could not spare the time nor had the patience to be investigated fully for her symptoms and I had great difficulty in making a diagnosis. With great reluctance, she was finally persuaded to be seen by a hospital consultant and investigations proved her to be much more seriously ill than either of us thought. She was found to be so anaemic that a weekly injection was ordered. Although I had to make time to give it to her it proved to be not such a hardship as the most suitable day for her was Friday. This meant my wife received a bunch of flowers to grace our home every weekend.

Mrs Nurse was a generous lady. I remember her giving me an envelope in 1972, the day before I was going on holiday, and making me promise not to open it until I was on the plane. I was going to Israel with the family, but to say that I purposely respected her wishes would not be truthful. I put the envelope in the inside pocket of my jacket expecting the envelope to contain a happy holiday message and promptly forgot all about it. I suddenly remembered it as I was sitting relaxed in the aeroplane. I opened it and found to my astonishment that inside the card wishing me a happy holiday was a hundred pounds in crisp, five-pound notes. I was dumbfounded. In 1972 the law was that each person going on holiday abroad was allowed to take out only fifty pounds as travel allowance. I already had the maximum amount with me! What my explanation would have sounded like to the customs officials if they had decided to search me I dread to think. They certainly would not have believed the truth!

As Mrs Nurse's condition deteriorated she - of necessity - demanded more of my time and attention. My visits to her became twice weekly. When she was no longer capable of doing manual work I visited her three times weekly. She still however struggled on in her business but left the making of wreaths and wedding bouquets to her niece Doris. She still kept the accounts and managed the business.

Besides work, Mrs Nurse had one other pleasure in life – cigarettes. She chain-smoked. At the time I smoked myself, I was therefore not able to pressurise her to give up the habit as much as I would have done under normal circumstances. The problem was that her illness was abdominal and in no way related to her smoking or her chest. I was forced to be a bystander and watch her smoke one cigarette followed by another. Her fingers were stained, not from the flowers that she wove into wreaths, but from the nicotine of the cigarettes that never left her lips.

Mrs Nurse lived over her shop. The living accommodation was on two floors; the rooms were large and luxurious. On the first floor she had a dining room, lounge and kitchen. The lounge was extremely well furnished; Persian carpets were on the floors and Tiffany lamps lighted the room. This was the room where I normally saw her until her final illness when she was forced to take to her bed.

Her bedroom was on the second floor. This room had a characteristic which I had never previously seen, and have never seen since, although I have been in practice for nearly sixty years. The heavy lined velvet curtains which covered the windows had envelopes pinned to the inside folds. Inside these envelopes were five and ten pound notes!

I found out the envelope phenomenon by accident. One evening she sent for me to give her something to ease her abdominal pain that had not been eased by the tablets she had been prescribed. I had no alternative but to give her an injection of morphine. She was in bed. She would after the injection shortly be asleep. I suggested to her that I be allowed to draw the curtains before I left, to darken the room a little. It was then that I saw the envelopes in the folds. She noticed my amazement. Her excuse for hiding the money in this fashion was that she did not trust her bank manager with her money!

One Saturday, in 1976, the telephone in our home in Brockley rang at eight o'clock in the morning. This was an extremely rare occurrence. I always took Saturday morning as my half day and the housekeeper at the surgery had strict instructions not to disturb me. The arrangements were - and had been for years – that another doctor did my visits on Saturday. When my wife, who had answered the telephone, asked me to speak to the caller I knew that there had to be something seriously wrong.

It was Arthur, Doris' husband, who requested an urgent visit to Mrs Nurse. I knew Arthur well because he had been a patient of mine since his demobilisation from the navy. He and Doris had lived in Bellenden Road near the surgery, but since Doris – Mrs Nurse's niece - had taken over most of the work in the flower shop they had moved to Bromley.

A friend of his in Copeland Road, almost opposite the flower shop, had telephoned him saying that the shop was on fire and fire engines were there. As he lived out of the area and did not drive a car he asked me to go to find out what had happened to his aunt. It was much quicker for me to go he said than to wait until he could make his way to Peckham. I simply could not refuse and left immediately. I was too late to be of any help. By the time I arrived at the shop the fire brigade was ready to leave and the salvage vehicle had already arrived.

The shop was flooded and there was an overpowering smell of charred and burned wood. The only occupant in the building was a policeman poking about the charred wood where the counter had previously stood. I learned from him that it was believed the old lady had smoked in bed and had accidentally set fire to the place. She had been found burnt to death on the first floor landing. It was presumed that, in her attempts to escape from the fire in her bedroom, she had fallen down the stairs.

Mrs Nurse had already been removed to the mortuary in the Borough and I was asked by the police to go and identify her. No relative, nor anyone who knew her, had yet arrived. The police said that, as I had known her so well, it would spare the relatives a sight they would never forget. They were right!

I went to the mortuary and it was a most distressing experience to see a lady whom I had known and admired *toasted, and roasted*.

On returning home from the mortuary, as my children had not yet come back from the synagogue and it was too late for me to join them, I said my Sabbath prayers at home with the smell of burning flesh and charred wood in my nostrils. When my children came home my wife served up for the family Sabbath dinner cold roast chicken, the skin of which had been nicely browned.

I ran from the room. I felt violently sick! I skipped that meal. Even today when I am served cold roast chicken my memory goes back to Mrs Nurse in 1976.

Stuck In The Millwall Turnstile

The prize of being a long-serving general practitioner in the same practice – I was in Bellenden Road for 45 years – is that I had the opportunity of treating the great grandchildren of some of my original patients.

One family I had been associated with both as doctor and friend was the Perry family. Mrs Perry, the great grandmother, was a pleasant extremely fat lady. A smile never left her face and she was blessed with a fabulous sense of humour. She was so obese – well over twenty stone - that I can never remember ever seeing her seated. I must admit that I became her general practitioner only at the tail end of her life. Her ulcerated legs gave cause for concern. My visits to her home were of necessity frequent, but I never left her home without having had a good laugh. Evidently her weight problem had been with her all her life; all her stories related to this fact. This remarkable facet of her personality, of being able to joke about her own disability, is the reason that even now I remember incidents which she spoke about which occurred nearly a century ago.

Of the many stories that she related about her problems, the one I loved best, was the one about her adventure on a very busy Saturday afternoon in the old Millwall football ground. She was an avid Millwall football fan. Although she could not afford to travel to their away games she attended all their games at the *'Den'*. She would rather have died than miss one. I am writing about the old ground before the move.

One Saturday afternoon, on the day of a special cup match, she went to the ground early to get a good standing position. Being fat, she liked to have something to hold on to. Next to one of the intermittent poles, which supported the stand seats of the more wealthy supporters, was her favourite position. She walked to the ground from her home in Marmont Road which was a distance of one mile, and was feeling just that little bit tired.

On this occasion tiredness and excitement merged so she did not pay too much attention to detail in trying to get through the turnstile. She always had to be extra careful. She had to manoeuvre her fat body sideways to get through. As she had performed the feat dozens of times it had become second nature to her. She did it automatically. Today she forgot!

It was a cup match. Other Millwall fans had noted the same fact; they too had turned up early. There was a crowd entering the ground, there was some pushing and shoving, the ground was filling up. As she stood in the queue waiting her turn at the paying-in desk her excitement boiled over. She wondered whether she would be lucky enough to get a good position to see the match. Getting through the turnstile was the last thing on her mind.

She made a fatal mistake. She attempted to get into the ground as she had seen everyone else do. She attempted to go through the stile - front ways. No go! She now tried to manoeuvre, moved herself from side to side, and attempted to get through sideways. This simply allowed the turnstile to get a firmer grip on her body. She had committed the mortal sin of pretending to the turnstile that she was a normal person - of normal girth. The turnstile remembered her girth. It was not going to allow her to forget that she was not. She now could not move her bulk.

The entrance to the ground was blocked. She was the blockage. Now placed in this position, it was possible that traffic would be possible only with removal of parts of her body. In the case of a baby who is having problems being delivered, forceps are used. No manufacturer, however, had yet had the foresight to produce a forceps large enough to extract a twenty-plus stone woman from a turnstile.

She was stuck! Not only was she firmly and truly fastened in the contraption, she was hysterical caused by the discomfort of being positioned in this position. The ministrations of the frustrated crowd waiting behind her did not help. The crowd waiting to enter had also turned up early hoping to get good positions. They were being thwarted by this immovable object, who was determined to prevent them doing so. The crowd was trying to do the impossible - push her through!

The kiosk attendant, who had been on duty on many Saturday afternoons when Mrs Perry had gone through his turnstile realised at once that there was going to be only one solution to the problem – force. He had used initiative and called the fire brigade.

The firemen arrived, removed the turnstile and cut her free. A tremendous cheer went up from the crowd when she was finally allowed into the ground.

She was rewarded by being given a free season ticket to the stand. It was cheaper for the club to provide her with this luxury than to wait for her to have a return match with the turnstile.

To Shop Before Mother Died ?

Patients often have strange ideas of death and dying. When Mrs Wheeler's daughter sent for me in 1965 requesting a visit to her mother saying that she was dying I was not terribly worried. The daughter telephoned at 8.30 a.m. requesting an urgent visit. I was rather puzzled that there was a request by telephone. I knew the family had no telephone, but a walk to the surgery would have taken her no longer than a walk to the telephone kiosk. The top of Crofton Road where they lived was after all only a stone's throw away from the surgery.

I was treating Mrs Wheeler - an eighty-six years old lady - for a gastric ulcer. She had been treated for some months and was improving all the time. She had been up and about when I had seen her on a visit the previous week. I had certainly not expected such a drastic change in her condition in so short a time. The message passed to me requesting the visit was precise. Mrs Wheeler had passed a black motion, had taken to her bed and was now too weak to leave it. Would Dr Crown call immediately as her mother would not be alive if he waited to call on a normal visit after he had done his morning surgery.

I already had enough experience to realise that in old age anything can be expected to occur suddenly, without warning, and this lady was already having treatment for stomach problems. On the other hand, I knew from my experience with this family that when an urgent visit had been requested nothing really serious had been found. On the one occasion when a visit had been really essential the daughter had propelled herself down the road at two o'clock in the morning to hammer on my door, and my whole family had been made aware of the urgency!

On hearing the reason for this visit, I had to consider the fact that perhaps the daughter was correct in her supposition that something serious could have occurred. Perhaps her gastric ulcer had burst! The daughter had made no mention of pain and this fact puzzled me. The other diagnosis was the obvious one - her ulcer was bleeding; this was the cause of the black motion. I debated all these facts in my mind and decided that, rather than give myself a gastric ulcer through worrying, to ease my conscience. I would visit her before commencing the morning surgery. My patients already in the waiting room would have to wait until I eased my feeling of unease. I have to be honest: patients who saw me put my overcoat on and leave the practice premises were not too pleased at the thought of the extra time that they would have to wait before they would be seen.

The old lady was lying in bed in a white nightdress. Everything in the room was white and ghostly. Even the curtains had an eerie look of ethereal blankness about them. Mrs Wheeler appeared to be cheerful and quite delighted to see me - nothing like the greeting which I expected. She told me with a sigh that she had unfortunately not achieved her ambition of living long enough to see her daughter suitably married and provided for before she passed on into the next world. She had passed a black motion. This was a sign that mortification had set in. Her mother, who had died at the age of ninety-seven, had told her this. Her mother had died of pneumonia, but it was the same in every case. In her own case it had obviously commenced in her bowels. As it was the first sign of death, she thought it right and proper that I should be notified.

She was now only waiting for the process of mortification to continue. As I listened to her, I had the feeling that I had been asked to visit only to verify the fact. Perhaps as a second opinion! If I cared to go into the next room with her daughter I would see the evidence for myself. She had kept the stool in a pot as proof.

There must have been some irritation in my behaviour that showed as I heard this bizarre story, that with its time wasting would make it a long and tiring day for me. The mother, with her attention devoted to the imminent visit of the angel of death, was obviously not aware of this. The daughter however was. She took me aside to the staircase to explain the reason she had sent for me as a matter of urgency. She wanted to know how many hours it would take for complete mortification to take place. How many hours her mother had left in this world. I stood in shock at her complete certainty that her mother was correct, and that the end was nigh. Her final sentence really floored me.

'Will it be all right if I go out and do my morning shopping before she dies?' she asked.

———

Naughty Naughty

In 1970 I was called out one Saturday afternoon, while on rota duty, to a very beautiful Jamaican nurse whom I had met previously several times in the surgery. She was a patient of Dr Cook, one of my partners, but I had never had an occasion to treat her.

It was a lovely hot June day when this visit was requested and as the nurse lived in a flat in Lausanne Road I could easily walk the distance if I wanted to. Dr Cook had many mental patients and I knew before I went that she was one of his patients.

I was not surprised on arriving at her flat when she opened the front door wearing her dressing gown. I was told that as she lived alone she had no one else to let me in. My housekeeper who had passed on the message told me that the lady had a sore throat and required an injection. What the patient had not told my housekeeper was that the injection she required was depixol for her mental state! This drug is given to psychotic patients but I did not know at the time that she was on this therapy.

I was asked on arrival to accompany her to the bedroom and readily did so expecting to examine her throat. How wrong I was! I opened my case to take out some spatulae, then what met my eyes, as I turned to the bed, completely stunned me. She had taken off her dressing gown and nightdress - and was lying on the bed completely naked.

'I know why you have come and what you want,' she said. 'Please get it over quickly, and don't hurt me.'

I am a coward. Perhaps it was her saying 'please' which threw me. I didn't know what to say or how to react. I just grabbed my medical bag and fled.

To my surprise Saturday evening passed without any further response from the lady but on the following day there was another call. This time I was told that she required a visit as she needed an injection of depixol. Though I had answered the telephone and taken the call myself she made no apology for the previous day's performance. She sounded quite normal and joked with me on the phone by saying that unless she had an injection she might do something abnormal and had to go on duty that afternoon in Greenwich Hospital. I can't explain why but I had the feeling that the previous afternoon's performance was an aberration, not in line with her normal behaviour, so I went to her flat again.

Once again she answered the door in her dressing gown but appeared to be completely rational. She made no mention of the previous day. Neither did I. I gave her an injection of depixol and fled in case she tried to tempt me again with her naked body.

I had no reason to see this nurse again as my partner returned from holiday the next day and took over her management. From him I learned that she was married to a normal fellow and he was having a hell of a life in coping with her abnormal behaviour.

Some weeks later Dr Cook told me that in spite of her beauty the fellow had decided to divorce her. A year later I learned that – in one of her attacks - she had set her flat on fire and was found dead in the blaze.

———————

George Fredericks, a seventy-two year old grey-haired gentleman, came into my surgery one evening in August 1979 as an emergency, to consult me about his *private parts*. He had lived with his mother and brother Joe in Lyndhurst Grove but, although I had treated his mother and brother on many occasions, I could not recollect ever having previously seen this fellow. His appearance was so distinctive I could not have forgotten.

He and his brother were bachelors, had been excellent sons and had spent their lives looking after the old lady. There was a married sister in the area, but I did not know her and from the old lady's description I was not missing much. The sister had appeared only on high days and holy days and at all other times had left the old lady to be cared for by her brothers. This arrangement had continued until the old lady died in 1976 and the brothers were then left to care for each other. I never heard either brother speak of a sister and would not have known of her existence if the mother had never spoken about her.

This first encounter with George occurred three years after his mother's death. He appeared at my surgery wearing a dirty wide trilby hat pulled well down over his forehead, a dirty long mackintosh, greasy trousers with turn-ups, and an old dirty crumpled shirt which looked as if it had never been washed. His shirt collar was open even though he sported a tie that from its appearance seemed as if it was as old as he was himself. On a peremptory look, his dress personified the picture of a dirty old man.

He told the receptionists that he was an emergency, needed to see a doctor urgently, but refused to say why or what the problem was that had brought him to the surgery. He insisted that he see me. I was his doctor. I was the one he would see however long he had to wait. The receptionist on duty had no alternative but to fit him into one of my emergency appointment slots.

He was sent to the waiting room which was situated in the garden and took his seat in the crowded room without making any fuss. When the patient I had been treating left my room and I called in my next patient my eyes could not fail to notice this odd-looking character, his bashed-up hat firmly ensconced on his head. I have to be honest, I called him in to see me before his appointed time. One reason was curiosity, I had known the family to be clean; this chap looked like a dirty old tramp. Another reason was that he stank out the waiting room; patients waiting in the room looked at me appealingly whenever a new patient was ushered in. Before his entrance we had both received dirty looks!

When I finally called him in I shook his hand and showed him to a seat. The question of a seat I had debated in my mind before his entrance. He was such an unkempt-looking character that I had thought when I called him in that I should keep him standing! I asked him for his complaints, but he first explained why he insisted on seeing me and not one of my colleagues. He knew me from his mother. She had frequently spoken about me and how helpful I was. He had been a porter in Covent Garden vegetable market all his life and had never previously been ill. He had been registered with me as an NHS patient for nearly twenty years and never once troubled me.

He explained that he had never had time to be ill. Apart from a weekly visit to the West End he had spent all his time and money on his old Mom. It was obvious from his first few remarks that he had worshipped the old lady; the care lavished on her probably explained why she was almost ninety years old when she died.

We now spent some time speaking about his old Mom for I remembered her well. She had been a tiny shrivelled up old lady, almost bent double by her arthritis. She shuffled slowly to the front door to open it. Her living room had been at the back of the house; a visit to her had always taken up a lot of my time.

George was friendly and communicative. Although we had never previously met his mother had obviously spoken to him a good deal about me. I was however running late, also out of patience, so I asked him what the real reason was for his visit. He didn't answer. He stood up. He peeled off his dirty mackintosh, took off a threadbare coat jacket, and unbuttoned the fly buttons of his trousers. He then produced, to my startled gaze, his penis. One thing he did not remove was his hat; this remained firmly planted on his head. For this I was grateful. To gaze on the jungle which lay under this canopy was something I feared. He had said not one word while this unbuttoning had taken place. To be perfectly honest, I had not paid too much attention to this unveiling. I had taken out a letter from his medical records and was reading it. A hospital consultant had written a report relating to some accident which George had suffered when a young boy.

George was the first to break the ice. 'Will you have a look at my *dick!* I think I've got VD,' he said.

I looked at him in amazement. Because his penis had irritated him on the previous day he had examined it and to his horror found a rash.

My retort was, 'you do not get VD from a lavatory seat: you should know better than that. Let me have a look. Anyway, what makes you think you could possibly have VD?'

Without the slightest embarrassment he gave me a history of going once a week to a French prostitute in the West End. Why he insisted on saying French I never asked.

He had been visiting the same one and only lady for twenty-five years. She was now in her fifties. When on the few occasions she had not been available, when she was on holiday for instance, she had provided him with a young French girl.

He told me all this while standing in front of me almost naked from the waist down. He was certainly a sight to behold. He stood with a trilby hat perched firmly on his head the brim of which almost covered his eyes, his shirt pulled up to his neck, and trousers wrapped around his ankles. His dirty well-worn underpants that had not seen the sight of soap and water for many months hovered midway between his buttocks and feet.

He suddenly spluttered out, 'I've got it! It's the young girl. She's the culprit. She's the last one I went with!'

He explained that Madam had trained the young girl in her early twenties so it was difficult for him to understand how he had caught anything. The ladies were meticulously clean and hygienic. They had always washed him down thoroughly before they allowed him to perform. From his appearance, as he stood before me, this last statement came as no surprise.

In the early years when he had first made use of the lady's services she had charged him two pounds. It was a lot of money in those days. As the years had passed she had increased her prices and two months ago she had increased them once again. It was now twelve pounds. Even this rate was a special one as he was a regular customer and an old age pensioner.

One thing he would not do, however hard I tried, was to tell me the exact address of his lady. He would say only that she advertised her services in the press and provided massage services both in her premises and clients' homes. Her workshop was a flat over a shop in the Leicester Square area.

He had a regular appointment - every Wednesday afternoon at 2.30 p.m. The time had been the same since he retired. He had come to see me on Tuesday. He had an appointment with the lady for the following day that he had no wish to cancel; this was why he had insisted on seeing me as an emergency. When he had been at work he had not been able to go during the week, his appointment had then been Saturday afternoon at 4.30 p.m. He had been allowed to use her services for exactly three quarters of an hour and was then politely shown to the door marked exit. Why he specifically mentioned an exit sign on her door I did not have the temerity to ask. I did not want to break the continuity of the dialogue.

Because of the journey from Peckham he was now always given a cup of tea and biscuit on his arrival. He had subscribed only to this one lady and was now treated more or less as one of the family.

I asked how he managed to get to the West End.

'Why, I use my bus pass,' he answered.

I had long since lost my irritation at the time I was taking in seeing Mr Fredericks, I was enjoying the narrative. I had already been in practice for twenty-seven years and had never met such a colourful character.

After giving me such a long history I felt duty bound to examine him thoroughly and he was delighted to hear that he had not contracted a venereal disease. His ladies had behaved impeccably; they could have had no influence on the diagnosis. The rash on his penis was due to thrush. Urine and blood examinations later confirmed the diagnosis that the thrush was due to diabetes.

Whether he went back to his lady to celebrate after I made the initial diagnosis of thrush I never had the courage to ask!

I treated him successfully for this complaint until 1991 when he suddenly went into heart failure and departed this life.

———————

One Saturday night, rather early one Sunday morning in January 1968 whilst on rota duty, I was asked to visit a patient who was not one of my patients. The group practice of which I became the senior partner had not yet been established and I had to drag myself out of a warm bed at 2.30 a.m. I had been woken out of a deep sleep and was not therefore in the best of moods. To add to my irritability and discomfort was that it was a dark, cold, rainy night. The temperature hovered around freezing point. The trees in Hilly Fields Park, opposite my home, appeared to be trying to keep themselves warm as their completely naked branches shook violently in the wind.

The request made to my wife on the telephone was for me to visit a child in the St Giles's estate opposite the hospital. The hospital has long since closed and been replaced by a residential estate. The hospital at the time was within walking distance of my surgery in Bellenden Road but not from my home in Brockley which was three miles away. My wife had been informed by the patient's mother that the child had already been allowed to suffer the pain of earache for three days and the parents were not prepared to suffer another sleepless night! This patient was not one of mine and I was feeling quite depressed at having to get out of bed. At that moment I hated the National Health Service, its demand that I work unsocial hours, and its lack of understanding in failing to reward me for doing so.

My car must have felt my mood. Not wishing to add to my distress it gave me no trouble in starting in spite of the cold and damp. It started immediately. There was little traffic on the road so in no time at all I was able to park my car outside the flats.

A smart well-dressed, short-skirted, heavily made-up girl in her late teens met me at the entrance. She had, I assumed, come to meet me to take me to the patient. I had noticed the girl's attractiveness even in the semi-darkness, but I thought her face would have benefited by not being so heavily plastered with make-up. I was not surprised at the girl being at the entrance to meet me. On night duty it was not unusual for a member of

133

the patient's family to be waiting outside to escort me to the patient. On many occasions when on being called to a lady who was being confined at home I had been almost dragged from my car by an anxious husband in a hysterical condition. I also remember the time when as soon as my car had stopped a husband had opened my car door - grabbed my maternity case and run - knowing full well that I would not be far behind.

The number of the flat I was visiting on this Sunday morning was nineteen. I had no problem following the relative up the stone stairway from the cheap perfume she was wearing and the clink clonk of her stiletto heels on the concrete stairs. Her perfume was obviously intended to be intoxicating as it wafted behind her in the enclosed corridors of the block. On this occasion she was wrong; it made me want to vomit.

This block appeared to be similar to the others in the estate. I had been into it on many occasions; many of my own patients were residents. The blocks of flats were old with winding staircases. As the landings were very dark the sound of this girl's footsteps was reassuring. I was not being made to search for the flat. The smell of her perfume, as it wafted behind her, also acted as a guide. While I could hear the clonking of her footsteps I knew that we had not yet reached our destination. The last thing I wanted to do at that time in the morning was to search for a number in the dark. I was grateful to the family for providing me with an escort.

We had now reached the fourth floor. Overweight, carrying a heavy doctor's medical case full of instruments and drugs, I suddenly felt tired and exhausted. This block I thought was certainly a peculiar one. In the other blocks number nineteen was certainly never higher than the third floor. What were we doing on the fourth floor? Perhaps I was wrong in the number. I had been given the number by my wife on the phone and written it down. I stopped to check the note on which the number of the flat to visit had been written. It was nineteen! I flashed my torch along the corridor and its light illuminated the number plate on the door of the flat to my right on the landing. The number stood out like a beacon, as if it was mocking me. It was thirty- nine! There was definitely something wrong.

My young guide – I could hear from the sound of her footsteps - had now almost reached the fifth floor. I dropped my case and ran up the steps to catch her. As I stood next to her, panting after my efforts to catch up, I was almost gassed by the intoxicating smell of her perfume. She had almost certainly bathed in the stuff. The heavy odour in that confined space took my breath away.

'What number are we going to, love?' I asked. My speech was coming in short pants from my exertions. When I recollect the incident she must have thought this customer is dying for it. He can't wait.

'What's it to you?' she replied.

'I'm the doctor on my way to do the visit which you requested,' I said.

She stopped. It was too dark to see her but there was no mistaking the anger in her voice.'

'What the bloody hell do you want to drag me up here for? You're no f.....g good to me!'

She roughly brushed past me. I almost fell as she rushed back down the stairs. This stupid girl had picked the wrong customer. For a few moments I thought I had revenged myself on my naughty girl because in her flight she crashed into my medical case that I had left on the landing. The swear words which were airborne in the passage and echoed through the block cannot be repeated. My joy however was short lived. She picked the case up and threw it down the stairs. I dragged myself slowly down the staircase and had difficulty in finding it in the dark passageway between the second and third floors.

Number nineteen was on the second floor.

────────

To make a living with a list of 200 National Health Service patients was no easy matter when I made the decision to be self-employed in 1953. The medical committee had already warned me that their decision was that I had to struggle with the tiny practice or never again bother to apply for one in London. I therefore accepted an offer in 1954 from Dr Godfrey, in the East End, to work for the night rota that he had set up. This rota consisted of ten doctors who worked in the Commercial Road, Mile End Road, and Silvertown.

The arrangements were that my duty would commence at seven o'clock in the evening but I would not be troubled until one of the doctors had a visit to do. To ease the problem of my having to make constant trips from Peckham through the Rotherhithe Tunnel to the East End a room with a bed was provided for me in one of the doctors' surgeries, when that doctor was on duty. I never had fewer than seven visits when on duty and never managed to get to bed until two in the morning. Even then, more often than not, my sleep was disturbed. Not knowing the area I would often get lost on my travels. The bed the doctors provided for me was a put-u-up, which I suppose was the best that could be provided in the limited space of the room. Nevertheless, as my last visit was always after two in the morning I fell into it exhausted. I earned the princely sum of two pounds per night for being on duty from seven o'clock at night until seven o'clock in the morning!

One incident I will never forget was when I did duty for Dr Cyderman in New Road, which is off Commercial Road, in Stepney. The elderly housekeeper had a flat on the top floor of the premises from which Dr Cyderman practised, and provided me with a space in one of her rooms when I was on duty.

At four o'clock in the morning in December 1954, I had been asleep for exactly two hours, when the housekeeper came into my room to wake me. There was a foreign sailor who required my attention and she stressed that he was a private patient. It was well known that these foreign gentlemen often used this surgery for their medical requirements. By word of mouth they knew that they could receive a penicillin injection for their venereal disease and often presented themselves for this treatment even though they did not have the complaint. Having had sex with a lady who frequented the docks they thought having an injection of penicillin was better than waiting for the disease to show itself.

The sailor, the cause of my awakening, was Portuguese. His English was most rudimentary and I now - over half a century later - still do not know one word of Portuguese. Our consultation was so fruitful that it took me a quarter of an hour even to find out what part of his anatomy he was complaining about. It suddenly dawned on my tired stupid brain that when he said piss he meant urinary trouble. I then spent another quarter of an hour attempting to extract from him by way of symptoms what the diagnosis might be. I was tired, his English was rudimentary, and I knew that he would never be allowed to leave by the housekeeper without something being done for him. To make matters worse, I kept slipping into German thinking this might help, but it only added to the confusion. On reflection he must have thought, this doctor is thick and I don't know why I am wasting my time in being questioned by him. Somehow, I finally managed to make him understand I wanted to know how long he had gone without passing water.

He answered, 'nine hours'.

I naturally assumed that he had come to see me as he had contracted some venereal infection so, with pornographic sign language, made him realise I wanted to know when he had last had sex with a woman. His answer was precise, 'woman, four days.'

His face suddenly screwed up with pain. He became pale, broke out in a sweat, and swayed on the chair. I caught him before he fell, and then half walked and half carried him to the examination couch. I laid him on his back and assisted as he took down his trousers. My intention was to examine him for urinary retention. I could not believe my eyes. He had a tight constriction in the middle of his penis and his foreskin was red and bulging, as if ready to burst. His penis was about three times its normal size and any movement of his body made his face crease with pain. This was obviously the cause of his urinary retention.

I advised him to go to hospital but the very mention of the word hospital brought a response. 'No! You help!'

On examination I found that the cause of the constriction was a curtain ring, which had been forced down to the middle of the shaft of his penis. The curtain ring could not easily be seen because of the swelling and I had to forcibly stretch the organ causing intense pain before I could determine the cause, and see the ring. He broke out in a sweat whilst I was examining him and I thought he might faint at any moment.

I once again advised him to go to hospital, but once again he adamantly refused. In broken English - whilst sipping water that I had given him - he explained that his ship was sailing for Sweden at eight that morning. He had to be on that ship at eight that morning! He cried. He begged me to help him. It was so pitiful to see him that I could not refuse to help.

It was not the first ring I had cut off. I had been a casualty officer in the Victoria Hospital, Blackpool in 1947-8, and had cut off rings. The trouble was, my previous experience was rings from fingers! We did have some luck that night. Although it took me over two hours to cut through the ring and remove it, this doctor's surgery was unusual in that it had a ring cutter. Luckily for him it also had a plentiful supply of Ethyl Chloride, a local anaesthetic, which helped to reduce the pain of the operation.

His story, in very broken English, which he told me as he relaxed on the doctor's couch after the successful operation, was that he had been held down by fellow sailors while the ring had been put on. He had tried to remove it himself without success; his efforts had only made matters worse. His actual words made sense. 'More I try, more ring on prick!'

I did not know whether to believe his story but the relief on his face after the removal of the ring was a sight to behold. He left me in ample time to make it back to his ship and I suppose in the circumstances his refusal to go to hospital was justified.

I could understand why sailors from the docks came to Dr Cyderman's surgery. The housekeeper never refused admission to them at any time of day or night. Presumably Dr Cyderman made a regular private income from these clients. I learned that she herself made a very profitable business from these visits, and encouraged them. She set the charges, the doctor just did what he was told. I was given to understand that she pocketed half the proceeds for herself. The doctor never handled money from the patient; he was never breaking any rules. She charged the patient what she thought appropriate and gave the doctor half the amount. The removal of the ring had cost the Portuguese sailor twenty pounds. This was an enormous sum of money in 1954.

I knew that I was going to get half of her charges. She always treated me fairly. I received ten pounds for my removal work that night, rather that early morning. For me a fortune! With my financial state being so perilous at that particular time I really could not have afforded to turn my back on the 'Lord of the Ring.'

―――――――

Out Of This World

It was 8.45 a.m. on an overcast, dark, dank, miserable January morning in 1987, the time when I normally set out from my flat in Forest Hill to drive to my surgery in Peckham. It had been snowing for a couple of weeks and there was a foot of snow on the ground. Public transport had been disrupted, train services had been cancelled, and the only means of travel in this part of London was the bus. Even buses went at a snail pace. It really was difficult to get about; people whose work was not essential were advised by the authorities to remain at home. Many did so, and found that their employers had other ideas: when they returned to work they found a day's pay had been docked for their absence.

I was unable to use my car because of the thick snow, and decided to make my way to the surgery by bus. This meant a walk to the bus stop opposite Forest Hill station, which is normally a ten minute stroll. Now, in the prevailing conditions, it would take me half an hour. Who cared? Everyone appeared so friendly; adversity often brings people together.

As I left my door I said, 'Good morning' to a girl who lived in the same block of flats. I had on many occasions raised my hat to her, but had never spoken. She was tiny; her little face showed through the mass of clothing with which she had protected herself against the elements. She smiled and attached herself to me. She too was walking to the station to catch a bus. I learned that the girl was Japanese and was studying English in the Honor Oak Language School. She now had no intention of letting me escape as she was obviously intent on practising her English. We chatted continuously as we trudged through the snow. Our main topic was Japan; we spoke generally about the country and how the weather in Tokyo and London were not so dissimilar. She asked my profession and when she learned that I was a doctor and had a son in Singapore she asked me why, when I had visited the Far East, I had never spent a holiday in her country. I explained that I had not yet been to Singapore as my mother, who had settled in Israel in 1966, had only recently died, and I had spent all my vacations with her. I told the young lady that she would understand my position, as the Japanese too were very respectful to their parents.

The girl stopped, horror struck! I was wearing a heavy overcoat, scarf, balaclava helmet, gloves, and Wellington boots. I also walked with a stick, to make me aware of the need to pace myself. I walked slowly and deliberately. I must have looked an old man. At that particular time, I was convalescing from a heart operation and as I hate the cold at the best of times I probably looked as though I was in my eighties rather than sixties. She turned abruptly and looked me full in the face. With her face only inches away from mine she blurted out, ' Your mother must have been very, very, very old!'

My heart problem had taken me completely by surprise; I had never previously suffered any symptoms relating to this part of my anatomy. On the way to visit Dr Healy, one of my partners in King's College Hospital who was recovering from a heart operation, I had suddenly felt a constricting chest pain while walking across the road. Lynn, the practice manager who had been accompanying me, insisted on my having an electrocardiogram before visiting our friend.

When we arrived at the hospital we found that Dr Healy could not be visited at that particular time as he was in the X-ray department. I therefore had no chance to prevaricate, just obey Lynn's instructions. I had an electrocardiogram followed by an exercise ECG on the treadmill.

Dr Healy had not been expecting me so the look on his and his wife's faces seeing me wired up for the treadmill on Storks Ward when they returned was of complete and utter astonishment. Storks Ward did have the dubious privilege of having both of us as patients in the following week. It must be some sort of a record for two partners, from the same practice, to be in the same ward, recovering from heart operations, at the same time.

To revert to my story of that January morning in 1987, I must have looked a sight to the patients in the surgery as I walked down the path from reception to my consulting room. There were one or two patients in the waiting room as I walked through, and I remember passing the remark, 'Thank God it's warm in here!'

I went into my room, took off my outdoor clothes and Wellington boots, and put on a pair of shoes. I was now ready for action. I put a stethoscope around my neck and prepared to commence my consultations. I opened the waiting-room door and beckoned Alvin to come in. I had known him over thirty years, ever since he had arrived in this country from the West Indies.

Alvin, a small balding West Indian man, always came in to see me in his best Sunday suit. He treated me with the greatest respect, even though I had told him on many occasions that he was a 'bloody nuisance'. He knew from my behaviour over the years that I had a soft spot for him. In spite of persistent backache, he did not come for medical certificates excusing him from work and had managed to work as a platelayer on the railway for over thirty years.

Alvin looked at me as if I was not there. He did not move.

Exasperated, I said ' Come in Alvin. You can come in now!'

He looked hesitant, dumbfounded and completely perplexed. He got up slowly from his chair and came into the room.

'What's up?' I asked.

'You're dead!' he stuttered. 'He told me you had a heart operation and died.'

'Who told you?'

'My friend Egbert.'

'What's wrong with being dead?' I asked.

I lowered my voice and whispered. 'Don't shout it out, Egbert is right: I died during the operation. They really messed it up. These hospitals are not the same as in the old days. They probably experimented on me knowing that I was a doctor and would never report them. They are a load of scoundrels. They know they can get away with it. They are always trying new things on doctors, hoping that they will work. You can't blame them completely, new treatment costs a lot of money so they give it to doctors first. The trouble is, it doesn't always work. Anyway, the problem we now have is that you had a heart attack last night and are dead too. It just has to be my fate to do casualty in heaven today and you have to turn up. You always had a lot of problems when you were alive. I suppose you have brought them all up here. I never have any luck!'

He had, when he had come into my room, plonked himself down in a chair in a state of collapse. His face was ashen. Except for his lips, not a muscle in his face moved. His body was limp. His eyes were glazed. He just stared into my face in utter disbelief. His lips trembled, no words came out.

'Why did you come to casualty?' I asked.

He suddenly appeared to wake up as if from a trance. His eyes wandered around the room. He was trying to recognize objects, but still did not say anything. His eyes fell on to an old army photograph, which had been taken when I was stationed in Crookham barracks in 1948, and which had been on the wall of my room for many years. This stimulated a reaction. He blurted out, 'You're joking!'

His brain and mouth however did not appear to co-ordinate. I could almost hear his brain ticking over saying, ' I recognise these objects, but I am not certain.'

The snow, falling again, gave the atmosphere an unearthly, eerie effect. The surgery was situated in a busy road, traffic was non-stop, and background noise was continuous. Now complete silence reigned. The effect was funereal.

'You are up to your usual tricks,' he stammered, still in a kind of a trance.

' Now look here,' I said. 'You are the one who said I was dead. You said so when I came in. I didn't volunteer the information.'

'I've got a terrible throat,' he said, in an expressionless manner.

He startled me. Whenever I had previously seen Alvin - over the years this had been several hundred times - he had always been multi-symptomatic. His head had knocked, his ears had buzzed; he had noises in his knees. In medical jargon he was a hypochondriac. I had never ever seen him so quiet and uncomplaining and have only one symptom. This behaviour of his was completely out of character.

I examined his chest and took his blood pressure. He still remained silent. His normal practice had been to speak all through the examination. I always had to tell him to shut up whilst examining his chest. A regular consultation had usually ended up by my having to stand up and open the door to show him out. He took up so much of my time with the multiplicity of his symptoms.

Not on this occasion! He took a deep breath when asked to do so and behaved like a model patient. I had never known him so quiet. I could tell from his reaction that I had not completely reassured him that we were both alive.

The stillness outside, no traffic in this normally busy area, had certainly helped to add to his discomfiture. I could see that he did not know what to believe. He had been so convinced by whoever had told him of my demise that my reappearance had been too much for him.

I now felt it was my duty to reassure him. After all, I did not want to frighten him to death!

'I was only pulling your leg as I usually do,' I said. 'I was only joking. I am not really dead. I was only kidding.'

He stared at me for several minutes. He was trying to remember something.

'You don't have to pretend to me,' he said. 'You really are dead, you know. Egbert told me he went to your funeral.'

'They must have buried another fellow. No one invited me to my funeral. Egbert has been pulling your leg,' I said.

He did not answer. He took the prescription I gave him, stood up, opened the door into the waiting room, and walked through it into the garden. He did not even stop to say goodbye.

I next heard a shout of pain and rushed outside. Alvin was limping down the garden path. He had kicked a wall to prove that he could feel pain and that he was still alive. He must have been so desperate to prove his point that he had kicked it with more force than he had intended. I watched him as he limped, moaning and groaning, to the reception area. He had certainly done some damage for he came back to the surgery the next day to see one of my partners about his foot.

He has never been to see me since that morning in January 1987!

He does not like ghosts!

142

What A Reception

Fred Smith stood on the patients' side of reception, mesmerised and transfixed. He appeared to be in a state of shock. The year was 1989, and how long he had been in that position I did not know. The weather was not that cold to have affected him, even though he was an eighty-six year old man. I knew him well as he had been a patient of mine for years. I had been treating this frail old man who lived in Nigel Road for eight years for his hypertension and benign prostatic hypertrophy. We were the best of friends and I could not understand why my greeting of 'Good morning', was being ignored.

I was standing on the staff side of reception with Lyza Edney and Ann Follett. They were the two receptionists, sitting at the desk at the counter between us, answering the telephones. I had said 'Good morning' twice, in my usual jovial fashion, with no response. I repeated the greeting two more times, before I realised that his eyes, on organ stops, were concentrated at some object behind me.

I turned. I then realised why he had decided to ignore me and concentrate on the item that had been of more interest. Sitting on a high stool, her legs crossed, white coat open, wearing a pelmet skirt, displaying more of her anatomy than Lynn - the practice manager – allowed, was sitting Vicky. She was the new receptionist who had been in our employ for only three days.

I was senior partner of the practice at the time but Lynn - our practice manager since 1972 who had been so successful in building up the practice – had full control of engaging staff. Lynn's motto was, 'reception is the window and first contact that patients have to the doctors', so the girls employed had to be young, intelligent and pretty. Lynn had contact with the schools so we had many girls who found that their first employment was in our practice. The girls were trained in the practice, and none of the staff who were in our employment before Lynn's arrival appeared to resent training the new girls.

Lynn had employed Fred Smith's apparition Vicky as a receptionist to replace one of the girls who had left the area. She had come for an interview dressed modestly and Lynn had been very impressed with her curriculum vitae. She had three good 'A' levels, was the daughter of a policeman, and lived not too far from the practice premises. On the first three days she had come to work dressed modestly, perhaps the white coat had hidden the skirt. Her face however had been normal.

What met my eyes, as I turned around to look at the object of Fred's organ stops, was not the girl I had seen the previous days. I had difficulty in recognising her. Perhaps her legs were causing our young eighty-year-old to be spellbound, but it was her face that fascinated me. It was ghostly white, with bright red lips. It was distorted. So many objects were attached to it that I lost count of the number.

I was told later that this new fashion our receptionist had adopted was called Gothic and was all the rage amongst girls at the time. Obviously this dress was not suitable for a doctor's surgery. The remark she gave when she was asked why she had become a nonconformist, and whether her father approved, was interesting. He had said,

'There is only one way to cure the condition - a stake through the heart!'

Lynn did not have to give notice to this girl. Vicky herself obviously found the employment not to her satisfaction and disappeared without trace, after a week. Interestingly, in the thirty-five years I worked with receptionists I can remember only one other lady who decided to retire without giving notice!

We were a family practice and worked in harmony. All the girls who left our employment invariably left to get married or leave the area. The receptionists were fun. Young pretty girls were an asset in that if at any time a patient was irate the sight of a pretty innocent face calmed the situation. It was only in later years, due to the problems and stress of the NHS, that it became necessary to add the older receptionists who had more experience in dealing with the more demanding patients. I can remember the names of twenty-one receptionists who worked in the practice at one time or another, but if any are reading this book and find that I have failed to name them please forgive me: they were obviously so efficient that nothing untoward occurred to disturb the calm of the premises in Bellenden Road.

Bernadette Quigley, a gorgeous looking girl, was Lynn's first young receptionist in our employment and her personality was such that we – the doctors – were convinced that Lynn was right in her decision to employ young people. She left us after many years to get married and all the practice attended her church wedding. The reception I will not forget in a hurry. It was held on a Saturday night in Croydon in the winter and my wife and I managed to go to the reception. I have met Bernie recently and, although she is no longer a beautiful girl, she is a beautiful lady with two beautiful children.

Another receptionist who was a character was Terrie Gosling. She was a pretty girl with a personality which even outshone her beauty. She was a real cockney. Not a day went by without something happening in the practice about her behaviour which did not give us pleasure. Denise Peacock, another receptionist, was never too particular about the way she wore her white coat. One day, Terrie, seeing Denise's coat caught in her buttocks, remarked 'Your bum is eating your white coat, Denise!'

Terrie left our employment when she married. On returning one day to visit her friends in reception, with her daughter who was about three years old, she saw me coming out of the practice manager's room. She turned to the little girl and said, 'say hello to your Dad!'

In all the years only one girl required to be told that her services were not up to standard. She had good reports from her school and was pleasant, but after a few weeks we found that our filing system and the girl were not the best of friends. It came to the point when Lynn said to me that she had to go and would I please be the executioner. This is where my *spiel*, which the good Lord blessed me with, came into play. I persuaded the girl that she was too good to limit herself, by her ability, to end up as a receptionist in General Practice. I had no wish to stand in her way. She had always said that she wanted to be a hairdresser; with her friendliness and talent she should reach the top. She agreed to leave at the end of the week and kissed me for my advice as she left the room.

One of my receptionists some years later met her in the street. She had tried hairdressing but had not found it interesting enough.

She was now a social worker for the local council!

———————

145

Rogues Solicitor

Mr Emmanuel Fryde, 'Manny', was an autocrat. He would never countenance any opposition to his dictatorial behaviour. He qualified as a solicitor in South Africa and having matrimonial problems there left to become domiciled in England. He never saw any reason to qualify in this country as he managed very well as the chief clerk of Sampson & Co., a law firm in the city. Most of the criminal fraternity went to Sampson's for representation and Manny ran the firm. He was the boss. London barristers' chambers were at his beck and call and vied for work that was high profile and financially rewarding. He was in the news all the time. On any day the Old Bailey would be occupying itself with several trials of his clients.

Manny was flamboyant - an extrovert. He was domineering in his behaviour but could be benevolent, if he was in the mood, and might benefit by so doing. He was superstitious to the point of stupidity and simply terrified of illness. He could be called a hypochondriac but this label did not quite fit his case. He never allowed his illnesses to interfere with his work schedule. He was a workaholic!

My first encounter with him was in the South East London District Synagogue in 1956 when he was keen to be elected on to the board of management and canvassed for my vote. Even though it was rumoured that his wife was not Jewish he was successful in being elected to the board. He became more and more outwardly religious. His real aim was at some future date to become a warden of the synagogue.

When he eventually did succeed in becoming a warden his religious fervour knew no bounds. He was selfish and irrational. A hypocritical farce intensified as he grew older by his fear that he was approaching his maker on the day of judgement. Whilst pretending to be pious in the synagogue, his bank manager spent Saturday mornings placing bets on horses which would be running at meetings taking place later in the day. This would take place even on Yom Kippur if there was a race meeting on.

He arranged for a *succah* – a booth for the festival of tabernacles – to be erected in the garden in his house in Pepys Road for the festival, even though he knew that he would not be using it. Although the festival lasts for seven days, he spent the time in his flat in Brighton – with no *succah*. He insisted that we knew about the *succah* by inviting (commanding) me, my daughter, the synagogue beadle, and the rabbi from Brighton to make a blessing in it on a cold dark damp night. Manny came especially from his office in the city for the five minutes we spent in it.

There is special blessing to be made in a *succah* when one eats or drinks something in it. Manny was not prepared to allow us to escape. It was pouring with rain. The *succah*, having just a covering of leaves for a roof, provided no shelter. We were drenched to the skin. Rabbi Fabricant, a genial fellow who should have made the blessing seated, decided to forego this obligation. He would have had to sit in a pool of water. We left like drowned rats. We were rewarded for Manny's piety with heavy colds!

One Saturday, at nine o'clock in the evening in the winter of 1968, the telephone rang. It was Manny, with a request for me to go to the West End Central Police Station to examine a client of his – immediately. A client of his had been arrested by the police and was being held in the police station having been charged with being drunk in charge of a motor vehicle. Breathalysers were not yet in use. The standard tests were to speak to the accused, check for slurring of speech, and ask the fellow to walk along a straight line.

When I arrived at the police station this man was sitting down in a cell, bent over, holding his head in his hands. When I asked him to stand, he stood up with great difficulty. He grabbed hold of me to steady himself and held me tightly around the waist. He then began to waltz me around the room. He would have fallen down had he not held on to me. The smell of his breath was so intoxicating I had doubts whether I would be sober enough to drive home! I was able to free myself only with great difficulty. When we both fell to the ground he broke into hysterical fits of laughter. I could get no sense out of the fellow. In my opinion he was blind drunk, and I telephoned Manny when I arrived home to tell him so.

He was disappointed. Could I possibly not find an excuse for this unfortunate man's behaviour? He realised that I had been disturbed on Saturday night when I could have had a visit to the cinema instead. If I could find some excuse for this man he would make sure that I was well rewarded.

My answer to him, 'it will shortly be Yom Kippur, my strictly orthodox upbringing will not allow me to lie in a situation such as this,' appeared to please him. He paid me such a small fee for this visit that I was glad I was never asked again to examine any of his drunken clients, even though I knew he had many more cases. He somehow believed that my attitude, and his acceptance of it, was smoothing a path for him to heaven. I learned much later that he used another doctor to deal with these drunken clients - who were small fry to a man in his position - and the doctor was prosecuted by the police for certifying a client to be drunk without even seeing the man.

To make sure the authorities upstairs were aware of his behaviour, he registered with me as a National Health patient. I stupidly accepted this heavy burden. I regretted it dozens of times but, to be honest, I was afraid to refuse. I knew that he had a vile temper and I would have upset him!

At lunchtime one day I was called to Sampson and Co., at their offices in St Bride's Street, to treat a racehorse trainer who was on a doping charge. I was told it was an emergency; the trainer had collapsed in his office. Manny had telephoned me personally from his office to tell me that the trainer was prepared to pay for the visit as a private patient. Manny could never understand that there were other patients in my practice who may have been in more need of my urgent attention. The trainer had indeed collapsed in Manny's office; his symptoms however were due to an attack of nerves. Whether the collapse was due to the fact that he was about to be charged by the police, or the charges he had to pay for the services of his solicitor for legal advice, I never bothered to stay to find out.

This visit was in 1970, and even at that time it was difficult to park in the area of his office in St Bride's Street, near Ludgate Circus. When I stopped my car in a no parking area, outside the door of his offices, I was surprised to find a traffic warden already standing there. I put my head out of the car window and asked him where I could park. 'Right here,' he said. He had been waiting for me. 'You won't get a parking ticket. Mr Fryde has asked me stay here and keep an eye on your car until you leave.'

Manny himself did not drive. He owned a car, but employed a number of chauffeurs. Whether he had ever driven in this country I never found out and would never have had the audacity to ask him. He bullied his chauffeurs unmercifully, but the pay and tips they received were so enormous that he made it worthwhile for them to remain - until his behaviour became unbearable.

I was summoned to his home one Saturday after midnight to witness his signature to a document. The document was an agreement between Manny and one of the Sunday newspapers to print the life story of Mr Wilson, one of the great train robbers. Whilst Biggs had fled to Brazil, Wilson had fled to Canada, and Mrs Wilson had returned to give Manny written permission for his side of the story to be printed. For these extra 'non doctoral' duties, whether it be by day or night, before leaving, he carefully placed a five pound note in the top pocket of my jacket for my services.

It was normal at that time for a criminal at the top of his profession, when apprehended by the police, to ask for Mr Fryde to represent him. I remember watching television one evening and seeing our Manny being interviewed outside Durham Prison where he had gone to defuse a confrontation between the warders and prisoners. He evidently had the respect of both the criminal fraternity and the police to be asked to mediate in such a dispute.

Most of the celebrated criminals of the time were his clients. The Kray brothers, perhaps the most famous, were amongst his clientele. I remember walking up the stairs of his house in Pepys Road late one night to attend his wife, who had one of her usual migraine attacks, and being introduced to two young gentlemen, in evening dress, who were descending. The 'gentlemen' were the Kray brothers who made the headlines of the newspapers in the following week. Although Manny led an active social life he never allowed it to intrude on his work and he had an office in one of the upstairs rooms of his house.

At his seventieth birthday party, held at the King David Suite, Marble Arch, the chief detectives of Scotland Yard Fraud Squad occupied most of the tables. He was on first name terms with them, from the chief downwards. During the evening he proudly introduced me to a man whom he had on that day successfully managed to get acquitted of murder. The man, accompanied by his wife, was in evening dress and looked as if he wished he were a million miles away. The couple knew that they were there as puppets at a show to prove how good Manny was at his profession.

His benevolence at times was obscene. This was demonstrated when he went on a group tour to Israel in 1970. He lost all reason. Like all Middle East countries Israel had its share of beggars who seemed to have a 'grapevine'. They were out in force at every destination to greet him. The tour group travelled by bus and when the bus reached one of the tourist sights the beggars were already waiting. They pushed, jostled, and bruised many of the occupants of the bus attempting to alight who stood in their path to greet 'our Manny.' They appeared to recognise him, even knew him by name! He stood on the bus steps like an eastern potentate and threw five pound notes, like crumbs to birds. It was not even the correct currency! He was so ostentatious. He thought that by behaving in this fashion, by this charity, he was buying himself a ticket to heaven.

His love of his fellow man, and his fondness for me, were demonstrated when he telephoned me one morning, about a year after his trip to Israel, to ask me to call at his home on my way to the surgery. When I arrived I found that I had been summoned to open a box of oranges, sent as a present by the speaker of the Knesset (Israel house of parliament). Manny was giving me the honour of opening the box, on the lawn of his garden, and had provided a screwdriver and hammer for the occasion. It was impossible for me to refuse such an honour. On opening the box I turned to tell him that it contained Jaffa oranges. But Manny was not there. I went into the house and found him cowering in the lounge behind the settee, some thirty yards from the box. He showed not the least remorse, as he proclaimed his friendship for me.

'Thank God! I thought the orange box might be booby-trapped I didn't want to get blown to pieces!'

Manny was an enigmatic character. He gave the appearance of being an observant and traditional Jew, but having divorced his first Jewish wife in South Africa he married a long-suffering non-Jewish lady in this country. She was placid, docile and amiable: a character in complete contrast to Manny. He dominated her completely and ruled every single action she undertook. The only reward for her subservience was to live in luxury. Another quirk to his character, which must have given her untold problems, was that he was a womaniser. I was once called to visit him in a public house in Deptford as he had contracted a urinary infection and I warned him about his extra-marital dalliances. His answer was, 'My prick has no conscience!'

Mrs Fryde already had a daughter from a previous marriage. This did not prevent him from taking charge of the daughter's affairs and that of the daughter's children too. In fact he took complete control of Mrs Fryde's family and gave them no opportunity to lead their own lives.

When Mrs Fryde's grandson married in Dulwich College Chapel, Manny insisted that many of his friends should be invited to the wedding, although they were unknown to the bride or groom. My wife and I were invited, but as Manny's doctor I did have some contact with the family, and did not feel strange in the company. Most of Manny's other friends did not know any of them at all.

The wedding must have been a distressing experience for Mrs Fryde's grandson Barry, and his bride, as he had already interfered with their wedding plans. Manny had 'persuaded' the college chaplain of Christ's Chapel of God's Gift at Dulwich, next door to the picture gallery, to marry the couple on the day of his choosing, and they hated him for it. They were married in the chapel. This was naturally their choice; they were Christians! They were then made to endure a reception and dinner held in the Café Royal, in central London, under *kashrut* (rabbinical) supervision. A rabbi who was a guest at the wedding even said the grace after meals – in Hebrew!

Mr Manny Fryde, being the piper, called the tune!

Mrs Fryde often related to me their experiences when they ate out. Manny had to give the impression of always eating kosher, so they spent a good deal of their time patronising Blooms restaurant, in Whitechapel Road. He was so well known for his generous behaviour, after he had drunk a few too many whiskies, that waiters waited expectantly for his arrival. When they arrived, so many waiters flocked around them that other diners would be neglected.

The waiters had played the scene so many times they had perfected the play. A waiter, on seeing the Frydes arrive, would be signalled to take himself to the nearest off-licence and purchase a bottle of whisky. They knew that they would be well rewarded for attending to this detail. After the meal, and a bout of heavy drinking, poor Mrs Fryde had the thankless task of fending off the waiters, as they came back for their third, fourth, and fifth five-pound tips.

His religious behaviour had some strange characteristics. He was never prepared to accept a contradiction, even when he knew that he might be in the wrong. This led on one occasion to a very hostile argument with a fellow Synagogue warden. A fracas developed after a Sabbath morning service when he called his fellow warden a 'low life'. Blows were struck. A lifelong enemy was made. He never forgot the scene, nor did he forgive the fellow warden, who was the innocent party. He carried to the grave enmity to people whom he believed had insulted him.

Another quirk in his character was his love of small birds. He had a budgerigar in a cage in his dining room. He treated this bird as if it was the most precious thing in the world. When I was called out to see him one morning I found the local vet from Lyndhurst Way holding the bird in one hand, and brushing it with a small paint brush in the other. With Manny out of the room I asked him what the diagnosis was. 'Nothing wrong with the bird. If the madman wants to waste his money by calling me out this week why should I refuse to come?' I nodded assent – I was in the same position!

On an occasion when I was called out early one morning he threw open the back door of his house to throw bread to the birds and anxiously waited for them to come and eat. The first birds to arrive were wood pigeons, presumably just to annoy him. He ran screaming into the garden, like a maniac, to drive them away. He became red-faced, speechless with rage. When I was present on a second occasion to witness the scene I rushed outside to calm him down and warned him of the effects that these birds were having on his raised blood pressure.

One lovely warm sunny afternoon in August 1972, I responded to a panic call to visit our Manny, in his home in Pepys Road. He was in a state of hysteria, and the house was full of police constables and detectives. He was running around the house like a man possessed! He had just returned from holiday and found, to his horror, that his house had been burgled. All Mrs Fryde's fur coats, including several minks, had been stolen. She was in no way as upset as Manny, but I could understand his distress. The thought that a criminal had robbed him when he was the criminal's best friend was abhorrent! He could not understand how anyone could have done such a thing to HIM.

I learned some time afterwards that a French gang, who were not clients of his and not subject to his whims and pleasures, had burgled him. One sentence however uttered by Manny on the telephone that day struck me forcibly. I had no idea who he was talking to but from the conversation it had to be one of the criminal fraternity.

'You don't have to go as far as that, you can let the bastards stay alive.'

It was the one and only time that I ever heard him swear!

There was a clean up in Scotland Yard in the 1970s. Manny decided it was healthier to leave the country post-haste. Before doing so, he went into hiding in this country to give himself time to remove files from his offices. Acting on a tip-off that his offices were about to be raided – his son-in-law was a policeman – he and an accomplice successfully removed vital evidence which they successfully burned.

He fled to Majorca and from there regularly telephoned me at the surgery for medical advice. He said that he did not trust Spanish doctors. I did not believe him. He just spent my time for free advice, double-checking on the recommendation for treatment he had been given. An occasion arose when he told me that the Spanish doctors had diagnosed prostate trouble and, as he was so insistent that he did not believe them, I lost patience. I told him that his symptoms, as described on the telephone, agreed with their diagnosis. His answer was, 'can you please arrange a private consultation with an urologist you know.'

'No problem,' was my reply.

I arranged an appointment with Mr Packham, at King's College Hospital, and Manny came over on his own from Majorca at Easter time and was sheltered by one of Mrs Fryde's relatives. Easter that year coincided with Passover, and my children who knew him well, will never forget his presence at our Passover Seder table.

He arrived at our house in Hillyfields Crescent, Brockley, on the first evening of Passover, dressed in a long overcoat, the collar of which was drawn up to his ears. He also wore a trilby hat, the brim of which was pulled well down over his eyes. If ever there was a suspect, he looked like one, dressed in this outfit.

Before he left our house at midnight he dressed himself up again in this same fashion, turned to my children and said, 'they won't recognise me like this will they?'

Who the they were I learned some years later. The they were the Regional Crime Squad and the Inland Revenue. There was an arrest warrant for him if he ever returned to this country and I have never found out how he managed to come back. He was diagnosed by Mr Packham as having prostate trouble requiring an operation, but returned to Majorca to settle urgent business before reappearing in this country.

He came back to have his operation in the private wing of King's College Hospital and I went to visit him on the first day after the operation. I searched the private wing but could not find him. I had received a message from Mr Packham that the operation had been successful and that Mr Fryde would be in the hospital about a week. I was so baffled that I went to the admissions department and was directed to the porter at the reception desk in the main building. By devious means, he had managed to get himself moved to a single room, in the maternity block!

At the time I was not too surprised. His wife had a few years earlier had an operation in this wing and I had visited her there many times when she was an inpatient. I knew that he had made his presence felt by all the staff of the ward and obviously knew what strings to pull to get himself admitted to that particular ward.

He told me that if they knew he was in England, and in King's College Hospital, they would not be able to find him. He must however have been the talk of every nurse in the hospital. The porter at the reception desk told me the number of his room without hesitation.

I went to his room in the ward but expressed no surprise at his accommodation. Knowing him as I did, the last thing I would have said to him was, 'Where is the baby?'

After the operation he returned to Majorca, where he lived for several more years. I had occasional calls from him before he informed me that conditions had changed in this country that allowed him to return safely.

I did not ask him what the changed conditions were which allowed him to return but thanked God that he intended to make his home in Brighton. He returned. As he was now too old to visit me, and my practice was too far for me to agree to be his doctor, I never had occasion to be troubled by him again. He lived only a short time in Brighton before his family informed me that he had collapsed and died.

His wife, who had been subservient to him in every way, followed him soon afterwards.

Salvation Army Officer Murdered

Major and Mrs Watkinson lived in Hooks Close, Peckham, in the 'seventies. They were a most affable and interesting couple who gave me an insight into life which I had never experienced.

Leslie Watkinson was born on December 19th 1928, and was called up for National Service in the RAF 1947. He served in Bomber Command, stationed in Huntingdon, and was discharged in 1949. He had been a steel worker before his service in the RAF so went back to the steel works on his discharge. He received a message that he had to help others. This made him accept a call to join the Salvation Army and he went into the training college in 1952. Here he learned that many and varied were the tasks performed by Salvation Army officers but their primary function was to act as full-time ministers of religion.

He was commissioned at a ceremony in the Royal Albert Hall, on Friday May 8th 1953, and his subsequent career was spent in men's hostels. He married in 1957 when he was a lieutenant. His wife was a serving captain in the Salvation Army but on her marriage lost her rank and now became Mrs Lieutenant.

Their first appointment together as man and wife was to a men's hostel in Frankfurt en Main, Germany, and what should have been the highlight of their career in the Salvation Army quickly turned sour. The hostel in Schifferstrasse 31 was not a brick built modern building, but an old Bunker. It was an air raid shelter that had been built of solid concrete, with walls about six feet thick and no windows. The whole place was a labyrinth of corridors, many of which were below ground level, and the single rooms were like prison cells. The electric lights had to be in constant use otherwise the place was in total darkness. The absence of windows obviously had a psychological effect both on workers and inmates. A spiral staircase reached to the top of the building and in the top there was a large room. The men ate and slept in this large room. Without windows, the *luftmachine* was essential to keep the air moving through the building. Living in these conditions was indeed a grim experience!

Lieutenant Watkinson's duties were mainly clerical and the issuing of stores, but he was also expected to conduct evening prayers and take part in the services on Sunday. He spoke German, but as his wife's knowledge of the language was limited, and she was in charge only of the laundry, she found the work difficult. The men who stayed in the hostel were homeless refugees; over a hundred men were accommodated.

The next posting was to 'Ostbunker', a similar type of place near the zoo, in the east of the city. This place was only an *'Ubernachtungsheim'* – a place where men could stay only overnight. This hostel was mainly for refugees in transit. The Watkinsons realised as soon as they arrived that it was to be only a temporary stay as they were there only to relieve the Officer in charge, Otto Zalewski and his wife Etti, who had gone on their holidays. As soon as Mr and Mrs Zalewski returned the officer again took command. As Leslie did not like the fellow and could not agree with the way he ran the hostel, they were allowed to return to Schifferbunker.

This move obviously did not please the authorities and they were posted to Stuttgart. By this time Leslie had had enough of living in hostels so resigned his commission and returned to England. He went into civvy street but the strain of leaving the Salvation Army was too great so he resumed his commission in 1967. He was posted to various establishments in Great Britain working for the missing persons department.

When I last saw him in the 'eighties he was working in the William Booth Training Centre at Denmark Hill, a stone's throw away from the surgery. He had been transferred from the missing persons department to work in the finance department. He told me at the time that he found the work boring and was remaining only as he was due to retire in 1993.

Unfortunately, he never reached retirement age.

He was returning home one day to his flat in Peckham when he was attacked and murdered.

May his dear soul rest in peace.

Horses Won

I had not been in practice in Peckham for long before I realised how important Mr and Mrs Hood were to me, both as patients and friends. They lived in Maxted Road, a stone's throw from the surgery, and were the apex of a pyramid of a very large family. Their importance, as we quickly established a relationship, was that they persuaded their family and friends to become patients of mine.

Mr Hood, a man in his eighties, was a descendant of a long line of bookmakers and seemed to know every racehorse including its birthday, its ancestors and how many races it had won. He knew every racecourse, every bend in the course, and which horse would be most suitable for a particular course. He had a library of books about racehorses and whenever I visited one of these books would always be open. These books fascinated me. They gave the ancestral tree of a horse and reminded me of my school days when I had to learn by heart the Kings and Queens of England.

Mr Hood's life had always been related to racing and his love of the sport continued until his dying day. I believe the only thing he did not know about horses, from his books, was the food they ate at any one particular time. I could even be wrong with this supposition! When visiting Mr Hood one day, my thoughts suddenly drifted back to 1951 when I had been an assistant in Newport, Monmouthshire.

I went to the synagogue every Saturday morning, and was accompanied part of the way home by Sid Joseph, the local bookmaker. He had an office in the main part of the town and our walk took us through the castle grounds. The castle benches were always occupied by the local gentry - run-down types - who spent all their time looking through the racing papers picking out winners for the afternoon race meetings. Sid was a character. He spoke Yiddish to me as we passed and, as all the turf fraternity sitting on the benches knew him, they greeted him. For my benefit he would make facetious remarks and he would smile as he acknowledged them with a wave.

'Du zest der mench' (you see that man) he would say, pointing to a tramp, *'her hut dus mihr gekaft* (he bought me this), and his hand would lovingly stroke the Rolex watch on his wrist.

One Saturday morning, as we walked through the castle gardens, he suddenly turned to me and said, 'put your shirt this week on Malka's Boy, in the Wokingham Stakes.'

I had neither heard of Malka's Boy nor the Wokingham Stakes, and was surprised that knowing my feelings about horse racing Sid had asked me to bet on a horse. He went on, 'you know, Isidore, that horse can't lose. Do you know what my mother's name was? Malka! I am Malka's boy.'

'You know I don't bet Sid, in any case I can't afford the money.'

'Never worry! It won't lose. It can't lose. If it does, I promise you that I will give you your money back,' he answered.

'In that case, I will ring you after Shabbat to put my bet on,' I said.

'No you won't. I won't take your bet. Ring up Shermans.'

I did as he said on the Monday and put a pound each way on Malka's boy, which was running in the Wokingham Stakes that week. Sid was right! The horse won easily at 100-7. On the following Saturday when I mentioned my good fortune to Sid he just smirked.

Returning to Mr Hood, on his deathbed - even though he was so dreadfully ill - he insisted that I put some money on a horse that he was certain would win. He had bronchopneumonia, was coughing up blood, but still had the sport's page of his newspaper open with the list of the day's race meetings on his bed. Because he insisted, to please him, I did something which I loathed, I got in touch with one of my patients, a bookie's runner, and put a pound on the horse.

One should always respect a person's deathbed wish. This horse did. It won handsomely at odds of 10-1. When I went back that evening to tell Mr Hood of my good fortune he just gave me a weak smile with a look of disbelief as though I could ever have doubted his judgement.

He never gave me another tip. He died that night.

Mrs Hood, a frail old lady, was also in her eighties. Eighteen months after her husband's death she contracted influenza and this was followed by bronchopneumonia. Treatment had not changed. And as she refused to be admitted to hospital I treated her at home as I had treated her husband, with twice-daily penicillin injections. Unfortunately her bronchopneumonia occurred in September, in the middle of the Jewish holiday season.

I am an orthodox Jew and as Yom Kippur was going to interfere with my daily visitation, I was at a loss as to know how I was going to cope with the situation. I told Mrs Hood that I would arrange for another doctor to call but she absolutely refused to hear of it. She would see no one but me.

We had built up a relationship of such trust, even in the few years that I had known her, that she simply refused to see my locum. We reached a compromise. I would give her an injection of long-acting penicillin before the fast commenced and I would give her another one on my return from the synagogue on the following evening. There was one proviso. She had to make me a solemn promise. She was not to die under any circumstances. If she did, I would never forgive her. She should remember that I was going to pray for her recovery!

When I appeared after the fast, she looked in better shape than I did. I had not yet eaten.

Her words of greeting to me were, 'You see, your prayers have been answered. I have done exactly as you asked. I did not die!'

———

Buying A Shirt

The Burtons, a large Jamaican family, registered with me as National Health patients in 1954. They were a group of men who arrived in this country in 1952 recruited for jobs that we British were not prepared to do. These jobs, so called menial ones, were for bus conductors, hospital porters and dustmen (refuse collectors). They were young and sexually active. The men not having their women with them found partners in Hyde Park who had sex with them behind a tree. The fee charged by the prostitute for the performance was the princely sum of one pound.

As the young men became more prosperous they deserted Hyde Park and were catered for sexually in their lodgings by a pretty Irish girl who was chaperoned by a white English pimp. The situation was an interesting one. While the girl was performing her services, the white Englishman spent his time in their lodgings selling them his Rael-Brook shirts, on the never-never.

The fellow was really a door-to-door salesman of shirts. He sold sex only as a sideline. The pimp took this girl to all West Indian houses where there was business to be done selling shirts and collars. At the same time he had the luxury of earning himself an extra pound, tax free, for every customer who wished to be serviced sexually. The girl was available only to shirt-buying customers. No purchase! No girl!

The only shirts he sold were Rael-Brook and they were available from him only on hire purchase. The girl was just a bonus, which gave him a tax-free income. If you were a customer you told the fellow when he called that you wanted the girl's services. You paid him a pound, and you took the girl to your room. Rooms were usually shared, so if your room mate was in he left the room for the few minutes you wanted to perform. Her pimp never left without an extra fiver in his pocket. How many houses he served in the same fashion they never found out. He would never leave without the girl. However hard these young men tried to find out where he lived - on several occasions they traced his movements for miles - no one ever discovered his office or hideout.

An interesting incident relating to the Burton family occurred in 1960 when they were drinking in a public house in Brixton. The family had by this time increased in number to include five brothers and several cousins who used to meet regularly once a week on Sunday morning, in this pub.

One cousin, Boysie, was white, and an argument developed one Sunday morning as to whose turn it was to buy the next round of drinks. The argument was a good-natured one, with much bantering, with the normal Jamaican sense of fun and humour, but which must have sounded offensive to people unaccustomed to the culture. Several black Africans happened to be standing at the bar listening to the argument, unaware of the family relationship.

In their opinion Boysie was being much too argumentative, authoritarian, and condescending to his black friends. He was speaking to the black men as they understood a white American from the South would speak to his slaves. They were not prepared to allow their fellow black men to be treated and spoken to in this fashion.

Boysie, a thin faced, blond-haired, albino, scrawny chap, was the only fellow of the Burton clan whom the Almighty had forgotten to provide with muscles. He must have weighed eight stone nothing. It did not take much effort for the Africans to lift him out of his chair and hurl him out of the pub into the street.

Surprisingly the incident had happened too quickly for his family to prevent. Retaliation however was swift and purposeful. Before the Africans had returned to the bar they were manhandled out of the public house, accompanied by kicks and punches.

They fled. They did not know that black men could sometimes have white brothers. It is only a matter of how much melanin pigment is in the skin.

Boysie was a lovely fellow. In all the years he was my patient we had a friendly relationship. Unfortunately, he is no longer with us.

May his dear soul rest in peace
